CURBSIDE

BY CHEF ADAM HYNAM-SMITH

CURBSIDE

MODERN STREET FOOD FROM A VAGABOND CHEF

BY CHEF ADAM HYNAM-SMITH

whitecap

Editors: Jeffrey Bryan, Jordie Yow
Design: Diane Robertson
Cover Design: Andrew Bagatella
Food Photography: Mike McColl
Food Styling: Adam Hynam-Smith
Typesetting: Andrea Schmidt

Printed in Canada

LIBRARY AND ARCHIVES CANADA CATALOGUING IN PUBLICATION

Hynam-Smith, Adam, 1980–, author

Curbside: modern street food from a vagabond chef / Adam Hynam-Smith.

ISBN 978-1-77050-223-9 (pbk.)

1. International cooking. 2. Street food. 3. Food trucks. 4. Cookbooks. I. Title.

TX725.A1H96 2014 641.59 C2014-903217-X

The publisher acknowledges the financial support of the Government of Canada through the Canada Book Fund (CBF) and the Province of British Columbia through the Book Publishing Tax Credit.

15 16 17 18 19   5 4 3 2 1

This book was printed on chlorine-free paper and made with 10% post-consumer waste.

This book is dedicated to my parents, Rob and Jill, for raising me the right way, allowing me the freedom to make my own choices in life, for supporting my early decision to become a chef, and for their continued support, passion, and pride.

To my Auntie Wen, for putting up with my drunken escapades while I lived with her during the early part of my time in Melbourne and for following my career with such passion and pride.

To my Nan and late Pa, for being there and supporting me without questions, and for teaching me the importance of family and honour. Pa, I know you're watching, so give yourself an extra helping of brandy cream. It's your birthday, after all.

To my Grandma and late Pop, for grounding me with stories of the family back home, and for your continued love and support.

To my brother, Cam, you little shit. I'm going to beat you in the next backyard cricket match. P.S. Collingwood sucks. Miss you, bro.

To my beautiful wife, Tamara, without whom this book would not have happened, for believing in me, supporting me and my decisions, and giving me a decent kick in the ass when I need it. Tam works harder than anyone I know, and the food-truck industry in Canada wouldn't be where it is today if it wasn't for her.

CONTENTS

FOREWORD

By Tamara Jensen

RUNNING A GOURMET FOOD TRUCK WITH YOUR husband makes for both a rewarding and challenging adventure on the road. For the first few years, I would spend most days on the truck bracing for a disaster. Blown brake lines? Fried water pump? We forgot to fill the propane? Again?! Anything can happen when your kitchen and dining room are at the mercy of so many forces, and after years of anything and everything happening, you learn to expect it.

But then one day, we're parked in the middle of a vineyard for a massive food-truck gathering with thousands of sunbaked, half-drunk street-food maniacs clutching their plastic wine glasses in one hand and smart phones in the other. After wobbling through the line, they celebrate their arrival at the truck window with a bellowing "I SAW YOU ON EAT ST.!" Our eight or nine staff, jammed on the truck, are hot and sweaty, dehydrated and exhausted, working as a well-oiled machine to keep the line waiting time down and the food photo-worthy and delicious. The expert food-truck festival goers know to order enough fish tacos and pickled octopus to share with eight of their friends, and we get cleaned out in a matter of hours.

When the food supplies dwindle, a few of us can finally escape from the 12 inches of space we've been allotted to do our jobs. Soon the chit rail, stuffed with customers' scribbled orders, is clear and the fridges are empty. Our staff, who are taking orders in front of the window, have lost their voices from yelling customers' names all day. They smile apologetically because we've sold out, explaining that a food truck only holds so much. We flip the menu board over, shut the window, and get to cleaning.

On this day, nothing bad happened. The water pump worked, our propane supply lasted, and the generator purred like a kitten. The best part? We could be proud of the food and our team, and Adam was happy with how the food tasted and looked as it went out the window. Maybe he yelled once or twice if the completely inexperienced friend we bribed into helping out with the promise of beer and tacos messed up an order, or someone in line asked if they could have their food gluten-free, dairy-free, and without the hot sauce (cringe). But in between the loud Aussie cursing that our staff has come to know and ignore, he would ask "Everyone good?! Everyone happy?! Who needs a beer?!"

Those are the good days. In four years of owning El Gastrónomo Vagabundo with Adam, there have been enough of those days to make it worthwhile.

Ironically, it was the loud Aussie cursing that got my attention on the beach in Barcelona in May of 2007. I had been backpacking through Europe with my friend Caroline. The Rivers Cuomo lookalike who worked the front desk at our hostel in Paris had recommended Sea Point Hostel for our next stop in Barcelona. After some room juggling that comes with never booking things in advance, I landed in a dorm room that, unbeknownst to me, was already home to a dozen reeking, drunk, sun-burnt backpackers on a birthday bender. As I would find out later that day, the obnoxious group of Aussies, Kiwis, and mixed bag of backpackers we had previously spotted on the beach were my new bunkmates.

"Hey, Canadian girl! Check out me sunburn!" I was unloading my backpack when Adam jumped down from his bunk after a mid-afternoon siesta, pink all over from the Barcelona sun. I recognized him as the loud one on the beach with the Aussie board shorts; the one who narrowly missed beaning a sunbathing tourist in the head with an Aussie rules football. He was grinning with drunken pride over his newly scorched beer belly, and stood there in his pink briefs (yes . . . pink) for the room to admire. It was love at first sight, or so I'm told.

A much less enthusiastic "Oi . . . Canada. Turn off the light," came from a bunk nearby. It was the birthday boy, Justin, and he needed his sleep before round two.

Fast forward to 2009. After living in Ottawa for a couple of years, me working in government cubicles, and Adam cooking diligently and begrudgingly under the thumb of restaurant owners, we had both had our fill. After researching the newly booming food-truck industry in the United States, weekly trips back and forth from Ottawa to the more temperate Niagara wine region, and gallons of indecisive tears, we took the leap and opened Ontario's first gourmet food truck in St. Catharines.

To say it has been an uphill challenge and steep learning curve is the understatement of my lifetime. I've learned a lot about food and business, and somehow we've even won some awards along the way. But what I've learned most is what attracted me to Adam on that beach in Barcelona: confidence comes from doing what you love, doing it well, and doing it with every fibre of your being. While working beside Adam—literally, beside him, crammed inside a used courier truck—for four years, his confidence has been contagious.

Adam's food is good. It's great, actually. I'm a cilantro convert because of it. I eat pickled octopus like candy, and my heat tolerance is through the roof from all the chilies I've scarfed down in recent years. You want your fish tacos without hot sauce? Too bad. Why? Because that's not delicious. There's no point eating something that doesn't taste good, and there's no point cooking food for others if it's not from the heart.

As long as Adam keeps cooking this food (and doesn't lose his Australian accent), I'm along for the ride with his vagabond ways, and I'm thrilled to invite you along on our journey!

INTRODUCTION

FROM AS EARLY AS I CAN REMEMBER, I ALWAYS wanted to be a chef. I grew up working in restaurant kitchens, starting at the age of 13. The kitchen environment is home for me; it brings calmness to my otherwise hyper personality. I love every aspect of the food industry, from the fish mongers and butchers to the servers, dishwashers, and my fellow chefs. Food and where it comes from is important to my everyday life, and I celebrate every meal.

Whether a dining experience is white linens and silverware or a milk crate on the side of the street, food and the act of eating has a very special place in my heart. I've been fortunate to work under some of the most talented and respected chefs in Australia, and to travel the world to experience the authentic cuisine and people of places like Morocco, Thailand, and Spain.

In 2009, I sidestepped out of the restaurant world to open Ontario's first gourmet food truck, El Gastrónomo Vagabundo. I have the freedom to cook the food I've learned to cook and eaten during my time in restaurants and travelling, focusing on globally inspired street food that showcases the best produce I can find.

It's one thing to watch guests in a restaurant dining room enjoying their meal from the safety of the kitchen, behind the pass; being a street-food vendor breaks down the barriers between me and my customers. I can watch the community buzz around outside the truck window, chat with customers about their day, and get immediate feedback on their meal. There is no better feeling in the world than a happy customer after their first bite of my food.

Since opening the food truck in 2010, I've realized that wearing two hats—restaurant chef and food trucker—has led to a blurring of the lines between what people expect street food to be and what I've grown up cooking in restaurants. The street-food scene has changed at lightning speed over the last five years, and the whole food industry has changed along with it. Customers now expect there to be fluidity and creativity in modern street food. Food-truck chefs have adapted restaurant-quality food to the street-food service model, and restaurant chefs have appropriated street-food dishes because of their popular appeal and ease of service. My food-truck menus are heavily influenced by my time spent cooking in top restaurants, and executing these dishes on the street is a rewarding challenge.

In this book, I hope to show what modern street food is from the perspective of an Australian restaurant-trained chef who has travelled the world and harnessed his culinary experiences to open one of the first gourmet food trucks in Canada. Street food in North America has come a long way in a short time and has proven to be an invaluable community experience shared by more and more people every day.

The modern street-food movement was largely spurred by the global financial crisis of 2008. People didn't have the money to spend on eating out like they used to. Things were tight for consumers and businesses. No one wanted to invest in high-risk restaurants with huge overheads. When we first conceived of our own gourmet food-truck concept in 2008, the food-truck scene in the United States was taking off like wildfire. Trucks like Kogi BBQ in Los Angeles were getting rave reviews, bringing attention to what street food could be and what trucks could offer.

Even before the financial crisis in 2008, fine dining was on the decline. Going out for a meal was more casual—you didn't have to tuck yourself into the table, so to say. Dining was becoming more communal, friendly. Restaurants scaled back on the linen and offered a casual environment where anyone could feel comfortable; that feeling of community and accessibility, coupled with really great, tasty food, is what defines the street-food experience.

When we conceived the idea and saw the popularity of the trucks in the United States—lines wrapping around the corner, zigzagging down streets—it was mind blowing. Social media was taking off, and trucks were showing up to lineups that were formed from a simple tweet. These trucks were taking it to the next level with their food and their business sense, and they inspired us to forge ahead with our concept and overcome the odds.

When we opened El Gastrónomo Vagabundo in 2010, we were one of the first trucks in Canada. There was progress being made on the West Coast, with trucks like Tacofino, and Roaming Dragon leading the charge. Ontario was a different story: street food still meant street meat—hot dogs and sausages, poutine, and little else.

From day one, it's been a steeplechase, one hurdle after another. We had everything stacked against us with the laws that essentially prohibited operating a food truck—or at least one that was actually mobile and actually served real food and wasn't just up on blocks in a gas station parking lot slinging fries and cooked-from-frozen burgers. In spite of our better judgment, we chose to ignore the hurdles and go ahead with our plan for a gourmet food truck.

In 2010, the local food vending bylaws prohibited us from cooking fresh food to order, and we certainly couldn't roam around St. Catharines. We worked very closely with the St. Catharines downtown city councillor, Mat Siscoe, and some very hardworking city staff to create a new bylaw that would allow "non-traditional" (translation: not a typical Canadian chip truck) mobile food vendors to operate on city streets. We received an outpouring of community support from residents and local business owners and presented a 60-page document outlining this support at a public meeting of the St. Catharines city council. We were blown away by the number and diversity of people who showed up to speak in favour of amending the bylaws, including local restaurant owners, lawyers, commercial real estate agents, and food-loving residents. Our proposed amendments were passed unanimously, making St. Catharines the first municipality in Ontario to adapt progressive street-food legislation.

Watching the street-food scene around the world, especially in the United States, and knowing that these hurdles could be overcome through honest hard work and sheer popular support reassured us that this thing could work. Respected chefs started to take notice of what diners wanted: something simple, affordable, convenient, and still high quality. Chefs opened walk-through windows at their restaurants, set up pop-up kitchens and market stalls, and opened trucks themselves. The trucks were a second source of revenue and a way of advertising the brick-and-mortar restaurant—a win–win scenario when every penny counts.

When you consider the street-food scene in places like Thailand or Morocco, and that it's been an essential part of everyday life and community for thousands of years, you realize the importance and value of the street-food experience. When you venture into the real, everyday culture of cities like Bangkok or Essaouira, you're exposed to a very different attitude than what we're used to in the Western world. You see it in the way people eat and the way the food is appreciated. There's gratitude for the food, the chef, and the vendor. Strangers chat amongst themselves, ask questions, and get to know their communities.

We've begun to see the same phenomenon with modern street food in North America. Strangers meet in food-truck lineups and at food festivals, talk about their favourite trucks and dishes, follow each other on social media, and interact in a genuine, meaningful way that, sadly, is a rare occurrence. Street food is bringing people together again.

My hat goes off to every street-food vendor who has worked so hard in their towns, cities, provinces, and states to overcome the same hurdles we've faced, and worse. They are not alone, and we are not alone. Every single one of these chefs, trucks, and vendors who weather the ups and downs (and the weather) inspires us to keep fighting the good fight and to keep on trucking.

ADAM HYNAM-SMITH

THE VAGABOND ROAD TO CURBSIDE

THE CONCEPT FOR EL GASTRÓNOMO VAGABUNDO began as a gourmet taco truck. I would take globally inspired recipes from my time as a chef in Australia and my travels and put them in a tortilla. They would be easy and fun to eat, and everyone loves a taco! The tricky bit is, I get bored quickly, and sometimes I just want to serve a beautiful plate of food the way it was meant to be eaten. So the menu has evolved over the years, and although we're known for our tacos, it's the more exotic, worldly dishes that are most rewarding for me to cook and most memorable for my customers. When I reminisce about my travels to Morocco and Thailand, specifically, my love for street food is renewed, and I'm inspired to cook something from my experiences in these beautiful, bustling countries.

VISITING MOROCCO

Moroccan street food is all about experiencing your community. From snacking on treats while you shop for fresh veggies in Jemaa el Fna in Marrakesh to sipping a mint tea with friends while you watch the fish mongers in Essaouira, it's all about being outside, catching up with neighbours and vendors, and enjoying the day.

I left Australia for Canada in 2006 and set up in Victoria, British Columbia. My travel plans were open, and so when my parents called and said they had the travel bug, we made plans. Mom and Dad wanted to go to France via Morocco, and I jumped on board. I spent two weeks travelling around Morocco with them, from Marrakesh to Fes, Essaouira, and Casablanca.

On top of it being an intense bonding experience with my parents—after working in kitchens almost non-stop from age 13, I hadn't spent this much time with them in years—it was the most memorable travel and food experience I've had to date.

My parents love food and travel as much as I do, so when my mom was planning our itinerary for Morocco, she set up a tour with a young chef. He took us to one of his friends' places in the lower Atlas mountains for a *méchoui* feast—a whole lamb slowly roasted underground in a pit of coals, served with vegetable tagines, fruited couscous, fresh-made breads, and salads. Everyone shared and celebrated as though it was the last time they would ever be with each other and eat this food.

We were in the middle of nowhere with a family that had invited us into their home with their neighbours. It was surreal. To be able to sit around a table with complete strangers and share the most amazing spread of food with people who ate this food every day but celebrated every bite was a life-changing experience for me as a person and a chef.

We stayed at a *riad* in Essaouira. I asked the housekeeper if I could help prepare the meal for that evening. I can't help myself from jumping in when there's food involved, and it was a chance for some hands-on training from a local that I might not get again. We went to the produce and fish markets, picking up lamb and sardines for tagines, vegetables and herbs for salads, and grains for couscous. Watching the way a Moroccan house cook put together an everyday meal was incredible. The little things, like the presentation, which we often dismiss in our Western home cooking, was remarkable. The way the average home cook in Morocco plates and presents food for a normal meal is artful and inspiring, and you can't help but appreciate and celebrate the meal.

After my time at MECCA, a modern Middle Eastern restaurant in Melbourne that has since closed, it was exciting to share the experience with the people who prepare it with love for their families every day.

VISITING THAILAND

Travelling to Thailand a few years later was life-changing. I could live in Bangkok or in a hut on the beach in Koh Chang any day. The kindness of the Thai people, the sense of community, and the undeniably fresh and delicious street food are, in essence, my happy place.

My now wife, Tam, and I travelled to Thailand in 2009 on our way back from Canada to visit the folks and tour Australia for a month. Between Toronto and Hong Kong, Tam came down with some kind of flu—she was, as we Aussies like to say, as "crook as a chook". At the Hong Kong airport, I practically dragged her to the connecting gate.

Tam curled up in a ball on the floor under the gate lounge seats, and I set off to find something—anything—to make her feel better. It was 4 a.m., and nothing was open on the concourse. I finally found a pharmacy-type kiosk and waited for it to open. I don't know if the pharmacist knew what I was saying, but he gave me a bottle of pills and held up five fingers, three times. I shrugged. When in Rome!

I trekked back to the gate and found a Canadian woman who was on her way to visit a friend in Bangkok looking after Tam. Tam gulped back some pills and spent the rest of the layover sweating it out.

I chatted with the Canadian woman about our travel plans, and she recommended taking a cooking class in Bangkok. It was already on our agenda, but we hadn't sorted out exactly where to go. Sitting nearby, an American bloke chimed in, "Go to Khao Cooking School, at the end of Khaosan Road." I noticed a cookbook on the seat next to him, flagged with Post-it notes and looking well-thumbed. The man noticed me checking it out and handed it over to me. "It's my latest book," he explained. I flipped through Chef Robert Danhi's *Southeast Asian Flavours* while he introduced himself. Based in the United States, Danhi was running culinary tours through Southeast Asia and was on his way to his wife's home country of Malaysia, via Bangkok.

Danhi began listing some street-food dishes I should try in Bangkok. "If you love coconut, you have to try *khanom krok*," he advised. These crispy, tender, coconut custard-filled pancake-like dumplings were already at the top of my list. Excited, I started telling Danhi about a video I had seen showing a street-food vendor making *khanom krok* during my YouTube-watching frenzy in preparation for our trip. "There's this guy who has a great series about street food in Bangko—". I stopped. Danhi was the guy in the videos. I knew he looked familiar!

We chatted until the plane boarded, me scribbling down places, dishes, and vendors to try based on Danhi's advice. I dragged a very groggy Tam onto the plane and off we flew.

When we arrived, I felt badly for Tam, who couldn't smell or taste anything yet. But that didn't stop me from eating. Every morning I would get up early while Tam rested and get my snacks from street-food vendors between our guest house and Khaosan Road. It became a ritual to sit in the gutter and

Top left: Dessert vendor, streets of Essaouira, Morocco. Top right: Fish monger at Essaouira fish market. Middle: Essaouira fish market. Bottom left: Tanners at work in Fez. Bottom: Our dinner being presented in the lower Atlas Mountains.

eat my breakfast. There was a friendly, smiling bloke I would go to daily for stir-fried beef and beans with chili and a fried egg on rice. I'd turn into the street and my eyes would burn from the chili vapours coming off his wok. The flavours and the smells would permeate the street, and I could already taste it. It was incredible. I would stand there and watch, chatting with the chef as much as I could while he cooked my meal, and then would grab a seat on the curb.

In this visceral, smelly, sweaty seat at the side of the road, you get a real sense of place and can't help but live in the moment while you're eating and people watching. The sights and the smells you experience while you're eating—fuel from scooters whizzing past; rancid odours from the night before coming from who-knows-what pooled in the gutters; the dense, humid, smog-filled air of the city combined with the fresh, eye-opening smells of food being cooked all around you—it's like nothing else. Five years later, I can close my eyes and the flavours, sights, and smells come rushing back.

After a couple of days wandering around Bangkok, Tam was up for a little more action. We stopped in at Khao Cooking School to check out what they offered. Chef Ajam Kobkaew, a motherly, kind-faced woman, ran the school with her daughter and another instructor. A busy woman herself—instructing students at a nearby university, liaising with the Culinary Institute of America, and appearing on a Thai cooking show—Chef Kobkaew rarely taught classes at the school any more. But she was there today.

I introduced myself and dropped Chef Danhi's name. "Oh! Chef Danhi! Yes!" Chef Kobkaew's face lit up. "You a chef?" she asked. "Yes, from Australia. My name is Adam." Chef Kobkaew was excited. "Chef Adam! Yes! I teach you tomorrow! Four dishes! Green curry. *Tom kha gai. Khao soi.* Pad Thai. Eight o'clock. All day!"

Even with the language barrier I could tell Chef Kobkaew thought I had a lot to learn about balancing Thai flavours. I thought I had a handle on balancing sweet, sour, salty, and hot, but Chef Kobkaew thought otherwise. She pushed me just past the point of my comfort zone. "No!" she would declare when I said there was enough fish sauce in the *khao soi.* "More. More!" I obeyed, and the result blew my mind. Although she still couldn't smell or taste much, Tam scoffed back the dishes, one after the other, eyes streaming from the whole chilies that peppered every dish.

Chef Kobkaew taught me to push the limits of the flavours of these dishes, and to trust my palate to find the right balance. My customers tell me all the time that the flavours of my food are like a slap in the face. "It's spicy, but, like, soooo good spicy!" I take it as a compliment, and I think of how proud Chef Kobkaew would be.

Top left + right: Learning the skills of Thai cooking from Chef Kobkaew. Facing page, top: Street-food vendor in Bangkok, serving braised beef shanks and offal. Bottom left + right: Bangkok street-food vendors and stalls.

TRIAL BY FIRE: THE STREET-FOOD TEST KITCHEN

At the inaugural Toronto Food Truck Eats, the first big food-truck festival in which we participated, we served hundreds of people, but it seemed like the line didn't budge. We were yelled at: "Bring more food! Bring a second truck!" People would come up from the back of the line and yell into the truck, "How long is this going to be?!" We started to notice that because people were waiting so long in line, they would order on behalf of a large group; one person in line might be ordering for six or seven people at once, which started to slow the kitchen down drastically. As this was the first food-truck event of its kind in Toronto, and the first for all of the food trucks involved, no one had any idea what to expect, and no idea how many people would turn up.

It took a lot of trial and error from event to event—changing the menu, the service style, the number of staff, the whole business model, essentially. You learn and you adapt to find the balance between getting the food out quickly while still offering something unique that has personality and skill behind it.

Customers and food critics have to remember that the food on any good truck is being cooked to order. It's not being held in a chafing dish or a steam table. It's the same as any good à la carte restaurant, only much faster and the truck staff can't distract customers by plying them with drinks at the bar. The food might not be plated with quite the same finesse, but when a customer orders his or her meal, the truck staff must have it cooked, plated, and handed out the window within three to five minutes or we'll read about it on Twitter for days. On the truck, we give ourselves that time bracket—if we can keep it under five minutes from when a customer orders to when they get their food, we're doing amazing. From the customer's perspective, waiting in line to order is one thing, but once they've handed over their money and they can practically taste the food they've ordered, time is of the essence.

As a food-truck operator, when I think about it, and I've got 100 or 200 people in line, and I have to have everyone's food out of the window within a few minutes of them ordering . . . Well, it gets very daunting when our team is cooking and plating to order and I look out the window to a sea of hungry faces with smart phones, ready to tell the world what they think of me and my food. Despite the time pressures and the risk of being slaughtered on social media, my focus always comes back to the food. Ultimately, it's about setting a standard for gourmet food trucks and for customer expectations, and about bridging the gap between food trucks and restaurants with the quality of food and service.

I've always prided myself on having an innovative food-truck menu, but none of the food has been served for shock value. I serve it because it's actually really good, and it comes from my favourite experiences in restaurant kitchens and from travelling the world. When I first put crumbed lamb tongue fritters and chili-mint relish on the menu, people would order fish tacos. And more fish tacos. I would ask, "Would you like to try the lamb tongue today?" and they would respond, "*Ewww*, no, I don't think I'd like that. I mean, it's tongue? Like, actual tongue? From a lamb?" So I would give them a taste. And an ultimatum: "Try the lamb tongue, and if you don't like it, you'll have to pay for it. If you do like it, and you eat all of it, it's yours on the house. Be honest." I gave away a lot of free lamb tongue that season, and since then, a lot of pickled octopus, braised beef cheek, and crispy pig's ears. In each and every instance, the customer has agreed that, yes, it is delicious, and, no, it's not as scary as it sounds. Having the chance to interact with and educate people about the food, the flavours, and the work behind the dish is one of the most rewarding aspects of food-truck cooking and street-food vending. My hope is that by sharing some of these recipes here, it will open even more eyes and palates to the possibility of street food beyond hot dogs and fries. A modern gourmet food truck is a restaurant kitchen on wheels, and there should be virtually no limit as to what can be served from it.

CONFRONTATIONS AND COLLABORATIONS

When we first opened, we felt massive backlash from a lot of restaurants; there were so many restaurateurs who got snarky and jumped on this wagon of negativity (no pun intended), telling everyone who would listen that we were stealing business and had an unfair advantage over expensive

Top left: Street vendor opening up durian. Top right: A street-food vendor in Chinatown, Bangkok. Middle: Khaosan Road, Bangkok. Bottom left + bottom right: Street-food vendors in Bangkok.

restaurant operations. In one memorable instance at a local farmers' market, a restaurant owner showed up at the truck window in the middle of a busy dinner service and berated us for taking his customers. I stepped off the truck, mid-service, to take the time to explain that this wasn't the case, that we actually have our own customers and people are drawn to our business for reasons that have nothing to do with his establishment. A few minutes later, a flash rainstorm rolled in, and all of our customers scurried off to seek their dinner and shelter inside nearby restaurants, including his. It couldn't have come at a more perfect time. I stood in the pouring rain and drove my point home by explaining to him that weather is just one of the many things that directly and immediately affect our bottom line. As the rain pissed down on both of us, and customers fled indoors, I looked him dead in the eye and cheekily asked, "Can I have *my* customers back, please?"

Fortunately, the naysayers have been a minority. There have been countless chefs who have stood by us, served their food at events alongside our truck, and provided a sounding board to figure out how to enlighten those suspicious of food trucks. We've collaborated with many well-respected chefs, inviting them on board the truck to feature a menu item and promote their restaurants while tapping into our customer base and social media reach; in turn, we've joined them in their restaurants to show off what we can do with a fully equipped kitchen, wine pairings, seats for customers, and protection from the elements.

Our good friend and food-industry colleague Paul Harber from Ravine Vineyard Estate Winery in St. David's, Ontario, has always been a rock for us. He has always put himself second in order to help us and many others with anything we need to succeed while furthering the industry. On countless occasions, I've sat with Paul at Ravine over a cold beer (yes, it's a winery, but chefs will always go for beer), just to have a chin wag and talk about where we are, what we can do, and if there's anything he can do for us. In the past, I've been near tears, ready to walk away from what we're doing, but Paul always says don't give up, everything will come together soon. Thanks to our hard work and support from people like Paul, it is coming together.

The collaboration between wineries, breweries, distilleries, and restaurants is a natural fit for the food-truck industry,

and a very important one at that. With the liquor licensing in Ontario and most other North American locales, food trucks don't have the luxury of serving alcohol. Pairing up with a wine or beer manufacturer or a venue that allows liquor sales means a win-win for both parties and a more complete dining experience for the customer. We experienced a prime example of this partnership during our most recent trip back home to Australia. While in my hometown of Melbourne, we visited a truck called Taco Truck, which was parked directly in front of a bar called Mr. Wilkinson. Chatting to the truck staff, we learned that the businesses had made an arrangement where customers who ordered food from the truck could use the bar dining room or the al fresco patio area to eat, on the proviso that they also purchased drinks. This partnership worked perfectly for both parties, and seemed to be a popular choice for the customers. They found a way for both businesses to benefit. All it takes is a bit of creative, friendly collaboration to make a special experience for the customer.

There is a strong sense of community and workmanship within the industry, and it's growing by the day. The result is an elevation of the standards within the food-truck and restaurant industries, and that's a win-win. Regardless of whether it's on fine china or a paper plate, it is, after all, all about the food and bringing people together.

STREET FOOD MOVING FORWARD

Over the few years that we've been open, we've seen massive progress in the acceptance of food trucks, and a real gratitude and appreciation that makes us feel like we've succeeded. We've changed bylaws to allow curbside vending and lobbied for food-truck permits in cities across Southern Ontario. Do we think that it's done and dusted, pat on the back, and we can sit back and relax? Not at all. There's still a lot of work to be done. We've merely peeled back the outer skin of the onion at this stage. Now it's time to put in the hard yards and make everyone aware of what this industry is capable of offering.

Top: My wife Tam's skillful menu board writing. Bottom left: Peller Food-Truck East in Niagara-on-the-Lake. Bottom right: Team El Gastró.

I'd love to see the powers that be in more North American cities get behind the food-truck movement. I hate the word "trend" or "phenomenon". Street food isn't a trend; it's a legitimate industry. It's always been here, from chuckwagons and taco carts to hot dog vendors and sugar shacks. It's just at a different level, and that's what scared people for some reason. It's risen up, and it's happened so quickly that it's caught some people off guard.

I want to see the real, hard work behind street-food vending exposed. I want the truth to come out about how hard working the chefs and vendors in this industry are. There are a lot of people in the restaurant world and beyond who assume food trucks make a killing. Maybe some do, and maybe I'm doing something wrong, but as far as I can tell, the little money you make for the massive amount of work you do would shock a lot of people. I want people to understand how hard street-food vendors are working behind the scenes to give their customers a plate of food and a unique experience. It's been glamorized, much as the chef industry as a whole has been, but there's so much more to it.

Here in Canada the winters can cripple your business. People see us with a huge lineup at these big summer food-truck events, but they don't see us parked at the curb in −4°F (−20°C) with barely a customer in sight for days on end.

We have to make this knowledge available, because the true appreciation for the food and the people behind the food is what will ultimately keep the industry going and growing. And getting people out, walking around and discovering their communities—that's what will keep communities going and growing together.

HOW TO USE THIS BOOK

The recipes I've shared here are adapted for serving at home, but they come from restaurant menus of my past, my street-food experiences while travelling, and from my own food-truck experiments with El Gastrónomo Vagabundo. Many of them have been served at some point or another from our food-truck or as street-food dishes in pop-up settings. These recipes have been tried and tested in some of the most difficult cooking conditions and by the toughest critics: hungry consumers!

A great place to start with this book is to choose a few recipes and build your larder or pantry. The *Mise en Place* section at the back of the book is your resource for spice blends, curry pastes, garnishes, and other components that are used throughout the book. Make a batch of hot sauce or curry paste, and you can use it right away or store it until you have a dinner party.

Some recipes are very straightforward, while others, like Pickled Octopus Tacos (page 193), require a little extra concentration and time. There's no better way to learn than to cook, and the more complicated processes in this book are detailed in a step-by-step fashion for you to follow.

Throughout the book, there are featured recipes from guest chefs whom I hold dear. These chefs are inspirational, and have been a source of support and camaraderie throughout my restaurant and food-truck careers. There's an old saying that it takes a town to raise a food truck—or something like that—and I felt compelled to pay homage to these industry legends who have been there along the way.

Some of the recipes here, like Battered Cod Tacos (page 177 and 181) and Tunisian Carrot Salad (page 30) are well-suited for serving family-style to share with company, while others, like the Crispy Soft-Shelled Crab with Pine Nut Skordalia (page 156), or the various ceviches, are plated individually to make sure everyone experiences the dish in an authentic way. In saying that, the important part of cooking and eating is to enjoy it with great company in an inspired setting, so have fun with the recipes and remember that there is no such thing as too many cooks in the kitchen . . . or on the truck.

Top + bottom left: The truck in service at Food Truck Eats.
Bottom right: Tam crossing off another menu item that just ran out.

SALADS & Starters

Since we opened El Gastrónomo Vagabundo, we've always worked closely with farmers in our area, on top of growing a limited supply of veggies, greens, and herbs in our own garden. I love salads, and love the contrast of colours, textures, and flavours that can be achieved with even the simplest selection of ingredients. We always make sure to feature a salad of some sort on the menu during the growing season, showcasing what's available from the garden that month. One of our favourites is the Heirloom Tomato and Watermelon Salad (page 25), which is constantly changing throughout the tomato season, with different ingredients and additions depending on what's available.

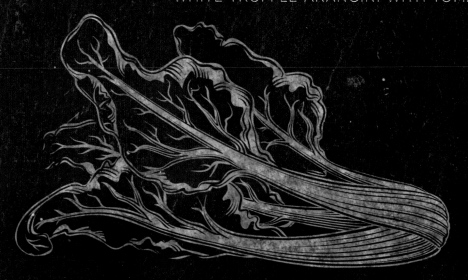

FATTOUSH

4 Pita Breads (page 254)

½ cup (125 mL) + 1 Tbsp (15 mL) olive oil

1 large red onion

juice of 1 lemon

½ English cucumber

1 avocado, pitted

20 cherry tomatoes

1 cup (250 mL) flat leaf parsley leaves

1 cup (250 mL) cilantro leaves

1 cup (250 mL) mint leaves

1 Tbsp (15 mL) ground allspice

½ cup (125 mL) red wine vinegar

¾ cup (185 mL) canola oil

3 cloves garlic, crushed

kosher salt, to taste

black pepper, freshly cracked, to taste

Fattoush is a Lebanese peasant "bread salad". Variations range with regard to the amount of bread used in the dish. This is a wonderfully fresh salad, perfect served on its own or with shellfish or seafood. I have served this from the food truck through summer when local tomatoes and cucumbers are at their best.

Preheat oven to 350°F (180°C).

Tear Pita Breads roughly into bite-sized pieces. Place in a bowl and toss in ½ cup (125 mL) of olive oil, being sure to coat bread evenly. Place oiled bread on a baking sheet and bake for 10 to 15 minutes or until crispy and golden. Remove from oven and allow to cool to room temperature.

Cut onion into ¼-inch (6 mm) wedges, lengthwise. Toss in a bowl with remaining 1 Tbsp (15 mL) of olive oil. Place in a roasting pan and cover with foil. Roast for 15 to 20 minutes or until translucent. Remove from oven and toss with lemon juice. Set aside and allow to cool to room temperature.

Cut cucumber and avocado into rustic, bite-sized pieces and place in a large mixing bowl. Halve tomatoes lengthwise and add to bowl along with cooled onion wedges, herbs, and allspice. Set aside at room temperature.

To make the dressing, whisk together red wine vinegar, canola oil, and garlic. Dress salad ingredients, and toss to combine. Season with salt and pepper. Add pita croutons and toss gently. Serve immediately.

→ SERVES 4 ←

BEEFSTEAK TOMATO, RED ONION, AND SUMAC SALAD

4 ripe extra-large beefsteak tomatoes,
  finely sliced crosswise
1 medium red onion, sliced into rings
3 Tbsp (45 mL) sumac
½ cup (125 mL) tarragon leaves
fleur de sel, to taste
1 Tbsp (15 mL) raspberry
  vinegar (approx.)
4 Tbsp (60 mL) sunflower oil (approx.)

This salad of tomatoes and onion is inspired by the tomato and onion sandwiches that my best mate, Ant's, mother Veronica would make us as kids. I always remember the hot summer days playing cricket and racing around like maniacs, then sitting down with a cold glass of water and a tomato and onion sandwich, with the smell of eucalyptus in the air.

On a large, flat serving platter, arrange tomato slices in a thin layer, allowing tomato slices to overlap slightly. Arrange onion slices evenly over the tomatoes. Sprinkle sumac evenly over the entire surface of the salad, and scatter tarragon leaves over top. Season with *fleur de sel*. Lightly dress salad with raspberry vinegar, and generously dress with oil. Serve immediately.

→ SERVES 4 ←

GLAZED HEIRLOOM CARROT SALAD WITH SMOKED CHEDDAR

24–30 young heirloom carrots
  (variety of colours), unpeeled
olive oil, for coating
1 cup (250 mL) honey
3 Tbsp (45 mL) coriander seeds, toasted
3½ oz (100 g) smoked cheddar
zest of 2 lemons
½ cup (125 mL) cilantro leaves
fleur de sel, to taste
sunflower oil, to finish

This dish is the perfect salad to serve family-style to be enjoyed on its own or as a side dish with anything from fish to beef or lamb. It is colourful and full of flavour, with a great crunch from the toasted coriander seeds.

Preheat oven to 400°F (200°C).

Trim carrot greens to 1 inch (2.5 cm) in length. Cut larger carrots in half, lengthwise. Rinse all carrots in cold water and pat dry with paper towel. Place carrots in a roasting pan and liberally coat with olive oil. Roast in oven for 10-minute intervals, tossing carrots in between, for up to 40 minutes or until al dente.

Remove carrots from oven and place in a large bowl. Add honey and coriander seeds and toss to evenly coat.

Using a vegetable or cheese peeler, shave the smoked cheddar into thin pieces. Set aside at room temperature.

Arrange glazed carrots on a serving dish and sprinkle with lemon zest. Garnish salad with cilantro and smoked cheddar shavings. Season with *fleur de sel* and dress liberally with sunflower oil.

→ SERVES 4 ←

GREEK SALAD

2 Tbsp (30 mL) red wine vinegar

2 Tbsp (30 mL) lemon juice

6 Tbsp (90 mL) olive oil

1 English cucumber, peeled and cut
into ⅛-inch (3 mm) thick disks

1 beefsteak tomato, halved lengthwise
and finely sliced crosswise

7 oz (200 g) Greek feta, large crumbled

4 red shallots, shaved into rings

24 kalamata olives, pitted and quartered
lengthwise

¼ cup (60 mL) dried *rigani*

½ cup (125 mL) flat leaf parsley leaves

> Greek or Bulgarian feta
> is available at specialty
> cheese purveyors and most
> Middle Eastern grocers,
> which is where you will find
> *rigani* as well.

Greek salad is a popular and fairly straightforward dish, so it's all about finding the best-quality ingredients when it comes to preparing this salad. Try to find really firm and salty feta cheese from either Greece or Bulgaria, and compose the salad artfully when you are plating it to show off all of the ingredients. Canadian "feta-style" cheese will do in a pinch, but I recommend looking for the real deal. *Rigani* is a Greek oregano with a specific flavour profile and should not be substituted with fresh or dried Italian oregano.

In a small bowl, whisk together vinegar, lemon juice, and oil. Set aside at room temperature.

In a large bowl, combine cucumber, tomato, feta, shallots, olives, *rigani*, and parsley. Dress with vinegar dressing and toss to coat evenly.

Arrange the salad on a shared platter or in equal portions on 4 serving plates. Serve immediately.

» SERVES 4 «

GREEN PAPAYA SALAD

½ medium green papaya, peeled
1 young coconut
¾ cup (185 mL) Thai basil leaves
½ cup (125 mL) cilantro leaves
¼ cup (60 mL) mint leaves
4 bird's eye chilies, finely sliced
¾ cup (185 mL) Nuoc Mam
  (approx.) (page271)
1¾ oz (50 g) dried baby shrimp
½ cup (125 mL) unsalted roasted
  peanuts, crushed
3 Tbsp (45 mL) Fried Shallots (page 250)
4 large kaffir lime leaves, spines removed
  and finely julienned

Young coconuts can often be found at Asian grocers.

Green papaya salad is perhaps the most popular salad eaten in Thailand. It can be eaten on its own or with different proteins such as pork belly, octopus, or fish. Green papaya is an unripe papaya with a white firm flesh. Although both green and ripe papayas have a green exterior, you can tell the difference in ripeness by the fragrant smell and soft flesh of a ripe papaya. Green papayas will not have a scent and will be very firm to the touch.

Cut the green papaya in half lengthwise, scoop out seeds, and then cut each section in half crosswise. Using a sharp knife or mandolin, finely slice papaya sections lengthwise. Finely julienne papaya slices and place in the bowl of a mortar and pestle. Using the pestle, bruise the julienned papaya to release the subtle flavour. Set aside at room temperature.

Using a sharp knife, carefully cut away the outside husk of the coconut and cut the coconut open. You can refrigerate the coconut water to drink later or drink it straight away. Using a spoon, gently scoop out the meat from inside the coconut, and cut any larger pieces of meat into smaller pieces. Place into a bowl, and set aside at room temperature.

Combine papaya, coconut meat, herbs, and chilies in a large bowl. Dress with Nuoc Mam just before serving.

To serve, loosely pile salad in centre of each serving plate and garnish with dried baby shrimp, peanuts, Fried Shallots, and lime leaves.

→→ SERVES 4 ←←

HEIRLOOM TOMATO AND WATERMELON SALAD

6 cups (1.5 L) basil leaves

2 cloves garlic

½ cup (125 mL) pine nuts

3½ oz (100 g) parmesan cheese, grated

1 cup (250 mL) olive oil (approx.)

kosher salt, to taste

4 medium heirloom tomatoes (variety
  of colours)

12 cherry tomatoes (variety of colours)

1 personal watermelon or ½ full
  watermelon

½ lb (250 g) buffalo mozzarella

fleur de sel, to taste

sunflower oil, to finish

6 sprigs tarragon, picked

6 sprigs basil, picked

We always have this salad on the menu through summer. The recipe changes slightly throughout the season. We add this, remove that, change this, but the tomato and watermelon always stay. Feel free to do the same, get inventive, and have some fun using the beautiful array of ingredients available to you.

TO MAKE THE BASIL PESTO, combine basil, garlic, pine nuts, parmesan, and olive oil in a blender, and blend until mixture is smooth but not thin, adding more oil if necessary. Transfer mixture to a storage container and season with salt, being careful not to over season. Cartouche the pesto by placing a layer of plastic wrap directly on the surface of the mixture, and store in the refrigerator.

Recipe will yield extra pesto, which can be stored in an airtight container in the refrigerator for up to 2 weeks.

TO PREPARE THE SALAD, allow tomatoes to come to room temperature. Scoop approximately 24 balls of watermelon flesh using a melon baller. Set aside at room temperature. Cut heirloom tomatoes into rustic wedges, and cut half of the cherry tomatoes into halves, lengthwise, leaving the remaining tomatoes whole. Arrange tomatoes and watermelon balls neatly on a serving plate.

Tear buffalo mozzarella into small strips and arrange neatly in the gaps between the tomatoes and watermelon. With the tip of a teaspoon, place tiny amounts of pesto in and around the tomatoes, watermelon balls, and cheese. Lightly season with *fleur de sel*. Liberally dress with sunflower oil and garnish with tarragon and basil. Serve immediately.

→ SERVES 4 ←

STIR-FRIED GREEN BEAN SALAD

1 Tbsp (15 mL) peanut oil
80 green beans (approx.), stems removed
¾ cup (185 mL) Chili Caramel (page 265)
1 small red shallot, finely sliced into rings
2-inches (5 cm) long piece ginger, peeled
  and julienned, divided
1 cup (250 mL) cilantro leaves, divided
1½ cups (375 mL) Thai basil
  leaves, divided
½ cup (125 mL) mint leaves, divided
3 Tbsp (45 mL) unsalted roasted
  peanuts, crushed
1½ Tbsp (22 mL) Fried Garlic (page 251)
2 bird's eye chilies, finely sliced
1 lime, quartered

This is a vegetarian version of a dish I would eat daily for breakfast in Thailand. It can be served family-style with roast pork or grilled fish. The combination of cilantro, Thai basil, and mint adds a flavourful freshness to the salad, while the ginger and nuts balance the flavours with a rich earthiness.

In a wok, heat oil over high heat. When oil is smoking, add green beans and toss for 3 minutes, allowing beans to become slightly scorched.

Transfer green beans to a bowl and dress liberally with Chili Caramel. Add shallot, half of the ginger, and half each of the herbs. Toss to combine, and place in the centre of a large serving platter. Sprinkle with peanuts, Fried Garlic, and chilies. Scatter remaining ginger over top, and garnish with remaining herbs. Serve immediately with lime wedges.

» SERVES 4 «

ISRAELI COUSCOUS SALAD WITH PEACHES AND ZHOUG

2 cups (500 mL) Israeli couscous

2 ears corn, shucked

1 cup (250 mL) mint leaves

2 peaches, pitted and finely diced

¼ cup (60 mL) sunflower oil

kosher salt, to taste

black pepper, freshly cracked, to taste

¼ cup (60 mL) Zhoug (page 274)

¼ cup (60 mL) Dukkah (page 237)

Israeli couscous, or *ptitim*, is a form of pasta that is toasted. It was invented to be a substitute for rice in the 1950s during a time of Israeli austerity. Israeli couscous, sometimes known as pearl couscous, is larger in size than regular couscous and does not clump together. This is a great salad on its own, or it can be served with fish or lamb, with a great contrast of textures and colours. The salad will not overpower the protein, but is flavourful enough to stand up to them without being overpowered itself. We served a variation of this salad during our first season of food trucking, and our customers ask for it every year when Niagara peaches are in season.

Heat a barbeque or grill to its highest setting.

Grill corn, rotating cobs so that the kernels are evenly cooked but not blackened. Remove from grill, and set aside to cool slightly.

Fill a large pot with 8 cups (2 L) of water, and bring to a boil over high heat. Add couscous, stirring initially to prevent it from sticking to the bottom of the pot. Cook for 12 minutes or until al dente.

Once cooked, strain couscous through a colander and rinse under cold running water until cooled completely. Drain well. Transfer couscous to a large bowl, and set aside at room temperature.

Using a sharp knife, remove kernels from cobs, and add to cooked couscous. Tear in mint, and add peaches and oil. Stir to combine, and season with salt and pepper. Set aside at room temperature.

To serve, mound equal portions of couscous salad in the centre of each serving plate. Dress with Zhoug and sprinkle with Dukkah. Serve immediately.

→→ SERVES 4 ←←

MARINATED CAPSICUM SALAD WITH CAPERS AND PRESERVED LEMON

8 red bell peppers

olive oil, to coat and to finish

½ medium red onion, finely sliced

3 Tbsp (45 mL) capers, rinsed
 and drained

1½ Tbsp (22 mL) Preserved Lemons,
 finely julienned (page 248)

fleur de sel, to finish

> This dish calls for preserved lemon, which must be made ahead of time as per the recipe on page 248. If you do not have time to preserve lemons, you can substitute fresh lemon zest.

"Capsicum" is the Aussie word for bell pepper. This salad is perfect for a tapas night with friends, and it is easy to prepare if you have Preserved Lemons on hand.

Preheat oven to 475°F (240°C).

Lightly rub red peppers with oil and place in a roasting pan. Roast in oven in 10-minute intervals, rotating peppers in between, for 30 minutes or until pepper skins blister evenly. Remove from oven, and place peppers in a bowl. Tightly cover the bowl with plastic wrap, and allow peppers to steam for 30 minutes at room temperature.

Once steamed, remove skin, stem, and seeds from red peppers. Cut peppers into 2/3-inch (1.5 cm) wide strips, and arrange peppers on a serving dish. Evenly scatter onion, capers, and Preserved Lemon over peppers. Liberally dress with oil and season to taste with *fleur de sel*. Serve immediately.

» SERVES 4 «

TUNISIAN CARROT SALAD

8 large carrots, peeled
olive oil, to coat and to finish
½ cup (125 mL) kalamata olives, pitted
  and quartered
1½ Tbsp (22 mL) coriander seeds, toasted
4 tsp (20 mL) cumin seeds, toasted
4 tsp (20 mL) caraway seeds, toasted
2 bird's eye chilies, finely sliced
1 cup (250 mL) cilantro leaves, divided
1 batch Harissa Dressing (recipe follows)
kosher salt, to finish

This dish is a classic Tunisian salad. This recipe is very much attributable to my former chef at MECCA, Cath Claringbold, although I have made a few adjustments, like leaving the spices whole to add another texture to the dish. This salad can be served on its own or is fantastic with fish or a grilled steak.

Preheat oven to 350°F (180°C).

Cut carrots in half crosswise and then quarter each half lengthwise. Using a knife, carefully cut the core from each section of carrot. Set core aside for stocks, soups, or feeding to the chooks.

Coat carrots in oil and spread evenly on a baking sheet. Roast in oven for 15-minute intervals, tossing carrots gently in between, for up to 45 minutes or until tender. Remove from oven, and cool on baking sheet to room temperature.

In a bowl, combine roasted carrots, olives, toasted seeds, chilies, and three-quarters of the cilantro leaves. Dress liberally with Harrisa Dressing, tossing to coat evenly. Season to taste with salt.

To serve, arrange carrots in a wood stack formation on a large flat serving plate. Garnish with remaining cilantro, and lightly dress with oil. Serve immediately.

→ SERVES 4 ←

HARISSA DRESSING

5 Tbsp (75 mL) Harissa (page 231)
1 clove garlic
3 Tbsp (45 mL) white vinegar
½ cup (125 mL) canola oil (approx.)
kosher salt, to taste

In a blender, combine Harissa, garlic, and vinegar. Purée until smooth. Transfer mixture into a bowl. Gently whisk in oil to combine. Be careful not to fully emulsify dressing.

Use immediately or store in an airtight container in the refrigerator for up to 2 weeks.

→ MAKES 1 CUP (250 ML) ←

BANGKOK PANCAKES WITH PAD THAI SLAW

BANGKOK PANCAKES

1 cup (250 mL) coconut milk

1 large egg

½ cup (125 mL) rice flour

1 cup (250 mL) all-purpose flour

⅓ cup (80 mL) palm sugar, shaved

4 green onions, finely sliced

1 Tbsp (15 mL) canola oil

PAD THAI SLAW

¼ napa cabbage, chiffonaded

¼ cup (60 mL) unsalted roasted
  peanuts, crushed

½ cup (125 mL) cilantro leaves

½ cup (125 mL) Chili Jam (page 266)

1 cup (250 mL) bean sprouts

juice of 1 lime

During my time in Bangkok, I was addicted to two particular street-food dishes: *khanom krok* and pad Thai. *Khanom krok* are little coconut tarts or waffles, and pad Thai is a sweet, sour, and spicy noodle dish known around the world. This recipe is my adaptation of both dishes into a refreshing and colourful salad that will put a smile on the faces of your dinner party.

In a large bowl, whisk coconut milk and egg until combined thoroughly. Add rice flour, all-purpose flour, and palm sugar. Mix well. Add green onions and mix to combine. Set aside at room temperature.

In a large bowl, combine cabbage, peanuts, cilantro, Chili Jam, bean sprouts, and lime juice. Toss to combine well. Set aside at room temperature.

Heat a heavy-bottomed skillet or cast iron griddle over high heat. Brush with oil to completely coat cooking surface. Reduce to medium-high heat, and ladle enough batter to create a pancake approximately 8 inches (20 cm) in diameter. Cook for 1 to 2 minutes or until the surface of the pancake bubbles. Carefully flip the pancake and cook for an additional 30 seconds. Remove from heat and set aside on paper towel to absorb excess oil. Repeat this process with remaining pancakes.

To serve, place one pancake on each serving plate, and neatly pile slaw in the centre of each pancake. Serve immediately.

→ SERVES 4 ←

CHILI CORN FRITTERS

kernels from 4 ears of corn

1 clove garlic

2 red shallots

1 kaffir lime leaf, spine removed

1 bird's eye chili, seeds removed

2-inches (5 cm) long piece ginger,
  roughly chopped

2 eggs

2 cups (500 mL) self-rising flour (approx.)

2 cucumbers, peeled and seeded

4 cups (1 L) canola oil

½ cup (125 mL) Chili Caramel (page 265)

¾ cup (185 mL) Thai basil leaves

These sweet, spicy, and aromatic pillows of goodness are one of the most popular dishes when I put them on the food-truck menu. They are a great snack for a warm evening in the sun when fresh corn is in season. Corn fritters are prepared in many ways around the world. This recipe is my take on a Thai-style corn fritter, using ingredients commonly found in Thai cooking.

In a blender, combine corn, garlic, shallots, lime leaf, chilies, and ginger. Purée until smooth. Transfer mixture to a bowl, and set aside at room temperature.

Crack eggs into a small bowl and whisk well. Add to corn mixture, and combine thoroughly. Add flour gradually to corn mixture, and mix to combine. Be careful not to over-work, as mixture will become doughy after cooking. Set aside at room temperature.

 Batter should be thick, similar to pancake batter. If it is too thin, gradually add more flour, stirring to combine between additions until desired consistency is reached.

Cut cucumbers into sticks approximately ⅝ inch (1.5 cm) in thickness, and 4 inches (10 cm) in length. Set aside at room temperature.

In a large pot, heat oil to 350°F (180°C).

Working in batches of 3 or 4 at a time, carefully drop tablespoon-sized portions of corn batter into hot oil. Deep-fry for 2 to 3 minutes or until golden brown and cooked in the centre. Remove corn fritters from the pot, and place on paper towel to absorb excess oil. Repeat as necessary.

On a large serving plate, arrange cucumber sticks in a thin, even layer. Randomly place corn fritters on top. Dress dish liberally with Chili Caramel, and scatter with basil. Serve immediately.

→ SERVES 4 ←

CRISPY TORTILLA CHIPS AND DIPS

CHIPS

4 cups (1 L) canola oil

24 6-inch (15 cm) corn tortillas, quartered

SALSA

4 ears corn, shucked

1 red onion, finely diced

½ cup (125 mL) cilantro stems and leaves, finely chopped

1 jalapeño, seeded and finely chopped

kosher salt, to taste

2 cups (500 mL) Guacamole (page 268)

¼ cup (60 mL) Smoked Pineapple and Habanero Hot Sauce (page 269)

Tortilla chips are so much better when you put the effort in and make them yourself. Serve tortilla chips and dips at a party for easy, flavourful snacking. Tortillas with salsa and guacamole is a common street food in Mexico; adding smoked pineapple hot sauce to the mix makes for a full-on mouth party!

In a large, heavy-bottomed pot, heat oil to 350°F (180°C).

Working in small batches, deep-fry tortilla wedges for 1 minute or until golden brown. Carefully remove fried tortillas from oil, and place on paper towel to absorb excess oil. Set aside at room temperature.

To make salsa, heat grill or barbecue to highest setting. Grill corn for 5 minutes or until lightly blackened on all sides. Remove from grill and set aside to cool to room temperature.

Once cooled, using a sharp knife, cut the kernels from each ear. Place kernels in a large bowl. Add onion, cilantro, and jalapeño. Season with salt.

To serve, place tortilla chips in a large bowl. Serve with Guacamole, salsa, and Smoked Pineapple Habanero Hot Sauce on the side.

→→ SERVES 4 OR MORE ←←

THREE-BEAN TOSTADA WITH GUACAMOLE

½ cup (125 mL) dried black-eyed beans

½ cup (125 mL) dried mung beans

½ cup (125 mL) dried black beans

1 batch Tarragon Dressing (page 272)

1 small tomato, diced

1 small English cucumber, quartered
lengthwise and finely sliced

1 small (or ½ medium) red onion, diced

1 cup (250 mL) cilantro leaves

kosher salt, to taste

1 batch Guacamole (page 268)

4 corn tortillas

1 cup (250 mL) canola oil, for frying

1 lime, quartered

A tostada is a fried whole tortilla with a dish plated on top of it. This particular tostada is one of the most popular items on our food-truck menu, and appeals to a variety of dietary restrictions, as it is vegan and gluten-free. If you like a kick of heat, add some Hot Smoked Pineapple and Habanero Hot Sauce (page 269) before eating.

Place each type of bean in a separate small pot. Cover beans completely in cold water, and bring to a boil over high heat. Reduce heat to medium, and simmer, uncovered, for 45 minutes or until tender.

 Be careful not to allow the pots to dry out as the beans will absorb a great deal of water.

Once cooked, remove beans from heat and strain. In a large bowl, combine cooked beans and approximately 1½ cups (375 mL) of Tarragon Dressing. Toss to evenly coat. Set aside and allow beans to cool to room temperature.

In a heavy-bottomed skillet, heat oil to 350°F (180°C) over medium-high heat. Reduce heat to low, and carefully place tortillas, one at a time, into the hot oil. Deep-fry until golden brown (1 to 2 minutes). Carefully remove tortillas from the skillet and place on paper towel to absorb excess oil.

Once the beans have cooled, add tomato, cucumber, red onion, and cilantro. Add remaining ½ cup (125 mL) of Tarragon Dressing, and toss to combine. Season with salt.

To serve, spread a generous amount of Guacamole on each tostada, and place tostadas on serving dishes. In a neat pile, carefully arrange bean salad in the centre of each tostada. Serve immediately with a wedge of lime.

→ SERVES 4 ←

EGYPTIAN EGG WITH ASPARAGUS AND CANDIED BACON

32 asparagus spears (approx.)

½ cup (125 mL) white vinegar

½ cup (125 mL) Tarragon Dressing
 (page 272)

kosher salt, to taste

12 slices Candied Bacon (page 249)

4 free-range eggs

6 Tbsp (90 mL) Dukkah (approx.)
 (page 237)

½ cup (125 mL) tarragon leaves

sunflower oil, to finish

fleur de sel, to taste

The Egyptian or *dukkah*-crumbed egg in this dish is inspired by a salad my former chef at MECCA, Cath Claringbold, would make. It's a *fattoush*, a Lebanese "bread salad", which she garnished with a *dukkah*-dusted poached egg. I've drawn on the classic combination of poached egg and asparagus and had a bit of fun with the rest of the dish. Since we brought this dish on to the truck menu in the spring of 2013, it has received a lot of praise and was included in a list of the best things eaten in 2013 on *Zagat Toronto*.

In a large pot, bring 12 cups (3 L) of water to a boil.

While water is heating, fill a large bowl with cold water and ice.

Sort asparagus into two piles—one pile of thick spears and one pile of thinner spears. Once water has reached a boil, carefully drop in either the thick or thin group of asparagus spears. Count to 25 seconds for the thicker spears and 15 seconds for the thinner spears, then remove asparagus spears from boiling water with a spider or slotted spoon and place immediately in ice bath to halt the cooking process and chill completely. Return water to a boil before repeating this process with remaining asparagus.

Once chilled, remove asparagus and pat dry with paper towel. Slice thick asparagus spears in half lengthwise and crosswise. Slice thin asparagus crosswise. In a bowl, combine all sliced asparagus, and set aside at room temperature.

In a medium pot, bring 6 cups (1½ L) of water and vinegar to a boil over high heat. While water is heating, fill a medium bowl with cold water and ice. Reduce heat to medium-high and bring boiling water to a simmer while dressing and plating asparagus.

Toss asparagus in Tarragon Dressing and season with salt. Arrange dressed asparagus neatly in a stacked wood formation in centre of serving plates. Place Candied Bacon on top of asparagus, arranged perpendicularly to create a stable bed for the poached egg.

Crack eggs individually into small dishes, careful not to break the yolks. Using a slotted spoon, stir simmering water in a circular motion, creating a funnel effect. One at a time, gently drop each egg into the centre of the funnel. Without boiling, gently poach eggs until the egg whites are soft but firm and the yolks remain soft. With a slotted spoon, carefully remove poached eggs from the pot and place on paper towel to absorb excess moisture.

Gently dredge poached eggs in Dukkah until completely coated. Place coated eggs on top of asparagus and bacon. Scatter plates with tarragon and dress liberally with oil. Season with *fleur de sel*. Serve immediately.

↠ SERVES 4 ↞

DOLMADES

1 Tbsp (15 mL) + ½ cup (125 mL) olive oil
1 yellow onion, finely diced
1 clove garlic, minced
¾ tsp (4 mL) ground allspice
¾ tsp (4 mL) ground cinnamon
½ tsp (2 mL) ground cloves
2 tsp (10 mL) fine sugar
½ cup (125 mL) uncooked short-grain rice
3 Tbsp (45 mL) dried currants
2 Tbsp (30 mL) pine nuts, roasted
1½ cups (375 mL) water, divided (approx.)
1 cup (250 mL) cilantro leaves,
  finely chopped
1 cup (250 mL) flat leaf parsley,
  finely chopped
1 cup (250 mL) mint leaves,
  finely chopped
20 large whole grapevine leaves
1 cup (250 mL) lemon juice

It is important that the grapevine leaves you use are free of tears, so that they are easier to roll and the filling does not rupture the dolmades.

To toast pine nuts, preheat oven to 350°F (180°C). Place pine nuts in a tray or a small pan and toast in oven, tossing occasionally until golden brown, 4 to 6 minutes.

From Greece to Bangladesh, Egypt, Iraq, and even Sweden, there are many variations on dolmades. This recipe is a Turkish take on the dish, filled with pine nuts, fresh herbs, spices, and rice. Dolmades are best served cold as a *meze* dish (a selection of small dishes, common in the Balkan regions), perhaps along with beet falafels, fresh breads, and dips.

In a medium stainless steel pot, heat 1 Tbsp (15 mL) of oil over medium heat. Add onion and garlic, and cook for 4 minutes or until translucent. Add dry spices and sugar, and cook until aromatic, approximately 2 minutes. Add rice, and gently cook for an additional 2 minutes, stirring constantly. Add currants and pine nuts and continue to cook for 30 seconds. Add 1 cup (250 mL) of water and stir to combine. Bring to a simmer, stirring occasionally so that contents do not stick to the bottom of the pot. As the mixture absorbs the liquid, add water ½ cup (125 mL) at a time until rice is al denté.

Remove from heat immediately. Working quickly, add herbs to the pot's hot contents, and mix well to combine. Transfer rice mixture to a large tray. Spread into a thin layer, and let cool completely at room temperature.

Once rice mixture is cool, carefully open grapevine leaves and lay flat, smooth side down on a clean work surface. Remove any thick stems from the vine leaves, and discard. Place approximately 2 Tbsp (30 mL) of rice mixture on the centre of each leaf near the base. Gently press the mixture together to form a neat, tight log approximately 2 inches (5 cm) long. Fold the outside edges of the leaf over the top of the rice mixture. Bring the bottom edge of the leaf up over the top, and start rolling to form a cigar.

 Do not roll too tight, as the rice will continue to expand. Set rolled dolmades aside. Repeat this process until all dolmades are rolled.

Preheat oven to 350°F (180°C).

In a baking dish large enough to hold all of the dolmades in one snug layer, place a layer of parchment paper to cover the base of the dish. Neatly arrange the dolmades in a single layer, without any excess space between them. Pour lemon juice and ½ cup (125 mL) of oil over dolmades. If dolmades are not covered by at least ⅝ inch (1.5 cm) of liquid, top up with water. Cover dolmades with parchment paper, and place a heat-proof plate on top to weigh down the dolmades. Wrap the entire baking dish with foil. Place in the oven and bake for 12 to 15 minutes or until the liquid has been absorbed and rice is heated through. Remove from oven, uncover, and allow to cool to room temperature before serving.

→→ SERVES 20 DOLMADES ←←

ZUCCHINI FETA FRITTERS WITH DILL LABNE

6 large (approx. 2.2 lb/1 kg in
  total) zucchinis
2 Tbsp (30 mL) kosher salt
  (approx.), divided
1 cup (250 mL) dill fronds, divided
2 large eggs, beaten
4 red shallots, finely diced
2 cloves garlic, crushed
7 oz (200 g) Greek feta, crumbled
½ cup (125 mL) all-purpose flour
3 Tbsp (45 mL) rice flour
black pepper, freshly cracked, to taste
½ cup (125 mL) Labne (page 270)
4 cups (1 L) canola oil
1 lemon, quartered
16 Pickled Radishes, quartered
  (page 242)

I used to prepare these fresh, pillow-like fritters at a restaurant I worked at in Melbourne. The herbs bring a robust freshness to the fried fritters, and the dill *labne* is a zesty, creamy contrast. *Labne* is made by hanging yoghurt overnight to form a cheese. It can be flavoured in a variety of ways, such as with the fresh dill in this recipe. When preparing the zucchini fritter mixture, it is very important to get as much of the liquid out of the zucchini as possible so that the fritter mix doesn't become too wet.

Grate the zucchini and place in a bowl. Sprinkle with 1 Tbsp (15 mL) of salt and toss to combine. Let stand for 15 minutes at room temperature.

Transfer zucchini into a colander and gently push to drain excess liquid. Working with small handfuls of zucchini at a time, place zucchini in the centre of a clean tea towel. Wring towel to squeeze out as much additional liquid as possible. Place squeezed zucchini in a bowl and set aside at room temperature.

Finely chop half of the dill and add to the zucchini. Add eggs, shallots, garlic, and feta. Mix well. Sift the flours into the zucchini mixture, and combine well without overworking the batter. Season with salt and pepper, to taste.

To make the dill *labne*, finely chop the remaining dill, and combine with Labne in a small bowl. Season to taste with salt and pepper. Set aside in the refrigerator.

In a large, heavy-bottomed pot, heat oil to 350°F (180°C).

Working in batches, carefully place tablespoon-sized dollops of batter into the hot oil. Deep-fry for 2 minutes each or until golden brown. Remove from the pot and place on paper towel to absorb excess oil. Repeat this process until all fritters are cooked.

Place fritters in a serving bowl, garnished with the lemon wedges. Serve the dill *labne* and Pickled Radishes on the side.

→ SERVES 4 ←

SON-IN-LAW EGGS

4 large eggs

4 cups (1 L) canola oil

8 sprigs mint, leaves picked

8 sprigs cilantro, leaves picked

8 sprigs Thai basil, leaves picked

1 red shallot, finely sliced into rings

½ cup (approx. 125 mL) bean sprouts,
  rinsed and patted dry

4 tsp (20 mL) Chili Jam (page 266)

4 tsp (20 mL) Chili Caramel (page 265)

juice of ½ lime

3 Tbsp (45 mL) Fried Shallots (page 250)

1 lime, quartered

We tend to serve Thai Son-in-Law Eggs as a breakfast or lunch dish on the truck. It is beautifully fresh, fragrant, and colourful. It is said that son-in-law eggs are served by a woman's mother to her son-in-law if she suspects him of mistreating her daughter. It is a not-so-subtle reminder that if he continues to misbehave, his ghoulies could end up fried on a plate like the eggs.

To soft-boil the eggs, bring a pot of water to a boil over high heat. Gently place the eggs into the water and cook for 5 minutes. Remove the eggs from the water and rinse under cold running water for 30 to 60 seconds. Peel, and set eggs aside at room temperature.

In a pot or deep-fryer, heat oil to 350°F (180°C).

In a small bowl, mix together mint, cilantro, basil, red shallot, and bean sprouts. Set aside at room temperature.

Place soft-boiled eggs into the hot oil and deep-fry for 3 minutes or until golden brown. Remove eggs from pot and place on paper towel to absorb excess oil.

To serve, place a spoonful of Chili Jam in the centre of each plate. Very carefully slice eggs in half lengthwise, and place cut side up on Chili Jam. Dress eggs and plate with Chili Caramel.

Dress herb salad with a squeeze of lime juice and garnish eggs with salad. Sprinkle with Fried Shallots and serve immediately with a wedge of lime.

→→ SERVES 4 ←←

WELSH RAREBIT AND PICCALILLI

RECIPE BY GUEST CHEF: DAVID WATT, THE GARRISON HOUSE, NIAGARA-ON-THE-LAKE, ONTARIO

1 Tbsp (15 mL) unsalted butter

1 Tbsp (15 mL) all-purpose flour

1 tsp (5 mL) hot mustard powder or
  English mustard powder

½ tsp (2 mL) cayenne pepper

1 cup (250 mL) black or dark lager beer

splash of Worcestershire sauce

1 lb (500 g) aged white cheddar cheese,
  finely shredded

1 small baguette

1 cup (250 mL) Piccalilli (recipe follows)

David Watt is the Executive Chef and co-owner of The Garrison House in Niagara-on-the-Lake and Zest Restaurants in Fonthill, Ontario. Dave is the grey-haired bandit of the Niagara cooking scene, and has a true skill and understanding of the gastropub concept. His food is diverse, flavourful, and honest. He and his wife, Leigh, have been vocal supporters of the food-truck industry and never hesitate to send people our way or help out in a jam.

This recipe is Dave's version of the traditional UK picante cheese melt, accompanied by a spicy and tangy pickled cauliflower. It's a favourite snack of mine, along with a few pints of cold beer, after busy evenings at the SupperMarket in Niagara-on-the-Lake, where we set up the food truck next to Dave's pop-up version of The Garrison House.

In a pan, melt butter over medium-low heat. Add flour, and cook for 1 minute or until fragrant but not brown. Add mustard powder, cayenne, beer, and a large splash of Worcestershire sauce. Stir well to combine. Cook for approximately 2 minutes. Gently melt cheese into the mixture, stirring to combine well. When mixture is smooth, remove from heat and allow to cool at room temperature.

Spread mixture evenly onto baguette and place under the broiler for 2 minutes or until golden brown.

Serve with a side of Piccalilli and a pint of black lager.

→ SERVES 6 TO 8 ←

PICCALILLI

1 small cauliflower, cut into ⅝-inch
  (1.5 cm) pieces
1 large onion, diced
¼ cup (60 mL) kosher salt
¾ cup (185 mL) white vinegar
½ cup (125 mL) malt vinegar
pinch of dried chili flakes
¾ cup (185 mL) superfine sugar
2 Tbsp (30 mL) English mustard powder
1 Tbsp (15 mL) ground turmeric
2 Tbsp (30 mL) cornstarch
½ English cucumber, peeled, seeded and
  cut into ½ inch (1 cm) cubes

Mix cauliflower and onion with salt and leave in a sieve placed over a bowl for 24 hours in refrigerator to draw moisture from the vegetables. After 24 hours, place cauliflower, onions, and cucumber in a resealable glass jar. Set the open jar aside at room temperature while you prepare the vinegar and spice mixture.

In a small pot, combine vinegars and chili flakes. Bring to a boil over high heat. Once boiled, remove from heat and allow to cool for approximately 20 minutes. Strain off chilies and discard, reserving vinegar.

In a bowl, combine sugar with mustard powder, turmeric, and cornstarch. Mix well. Pour one-quarter of vinegar mixture onto dry ingredients and mix thoroughly. Re-boil remaining vinegar in a pot over high heat. Remove from heat, and whisk vinegar into the wet sugar mixture. Transfer vinegar-sugar mixture to a pot, bring to a boil over high heat, and then reduce heat to medium-high and simmer for approximately 3 minutes. Pour vinegar mixture over cauliflower, onions, and cucumber, and set aside at room temperature to cool.

Serve immediately or seal jar and store for up to 3 months in the refrigerator.

→→ MAKES 4 CUPS (1 L) ←←

WHITE TRUFFLE ARANCINI WITH TOMATO FONDUE

RECIPE BY GUEST CHEF: ERIK PEACOCK, WELLINGTON COURT RESTAURANT, ST. CATHARINES, ONTARIO

1 batch Tomato Fondue (recipe follows)

RISOTTO

4 cups (1 L) chicken broth, divided

3 Tbsp (45 mL) unsalted butter, divided

1 Tbsp (15 mL) olive oil

½ yellow onion, minced

1¼ cups (310 mL) Arborio rice

½ cup (125 mL) white wine

2 Tbsp (30 mL) white truffle oil

⅓ cup (80 mL) parmesan cheese, grated

1 tsp (5 mL) milk (approx.)

kosher salt, to taste

black pepper, freshly cracked, to taste

½ cup (125 mL) flat leaf parsley leaves, finely chiffonaded

ARANCINI

7 oz (200 g) mozzarella cheese

4 large eggs

¾ cup (185 mL) whole milk

2 cups (500 mL) all-purpose flour

3 cups (750 mL) panko bread crumbs

4 cups (1 L) canola oil

3 cups (750 mL) basil leaves

Erik Peacock is the Executive Chef and Owner of Wellington Court Restaurant in St. Catharines, Ontario. Erik has been supportive since before we moved to Niagara from Ottawa. He welcomed us with open arms, and gave us valuable insight into the hospitality industry in Niagara. We invited Erik to participate as a pop-up vendor at the first Food Truck Eats event in downtown St. Catharines, and he sold out of these tender, deep-fried risotto balls in record time.

Prepare Tomato Fondue.

RISOTTO

Heat broth in a stockpot over medium-low heat for 5 minutes or until warmed.

In a large, heavy-bottomed pan, heat 1 Tbsp (15 mL) of butter and olive oil over medium-high heat. Add onion and cook, stirring, for 2 minutes or until translucent. Add rice and stir to coat. Cook, stirring, for 1 minute or until fragrant.

Pour wine into rice mixture, and cook, stirring, for 5 minutes or until liquid is absorbed. Add ½ cup (125 mL) of hot broth and cook, stirring constantly, until broth is absorbed. Continue this process, adding ½ cup (125 mL) of broth at a time until rice is tender but firm to the bite, 20 to 30 minutes.

Remove from heat and immediately mix in remaining 2 Tbsp (30 mL) of butter, truffle oil, parmesan, and milk until fully incorporated. Season with salt, pepper, and parsley. Spread rice mixture thinly across a large baking sheet and allow to cool completely at room temperature.

ARANCINI

Cut mozzarella into 30 equal pieces.

Form the cooled rice mixture into balls, pressing a piece of mozzarella into the center of each ball.

In a small bowl, whisk together eggs and milk until combined. Place flour and panko in separate bowls. Arrange your crumbing station in the following order: flour, egg mixture, panko.

As an option, you can further garnish with a light dressing of truffle oil and shaved parmesan cheese. And if you want to really toff it up, you can shave fresh truffles over the top!

Working with a couple of balls at a time, lightly coat with flour. Transfer balls from the flour to the egg mixture and allow to sit for approximately 30 seconds. Transfer the balls to the panko, and toss to coat the balls. Set aside in the refrigerator.

When ready to serve, heat oil in a large pot to 350°F (180°C).

Gently warm Tomato Fondue over low heat.

Working with a couple of balls at a time, carefully place them in the hot oil and deep-fry for 3 to 4 minutes or until golden brown. Using a spider or slotted spoon, remove from pot and place on paper towel to absorb excess oil. Repeat this process until all balls are cooked.

Place equal portions of *arancini* in the center of each serving plate. Lightly sauce with warmed Tomato Fondue, and garnish with basil.

→ MAKES 30 ARANCINI ←

TOMATO FONDUE

1½ Tbsp (22 mL) unsalted butter
½ large white onion, minced
2 28-oz cans (1½ L) superb-quality Roma
  tomatoes (drained of most of the juice)
½ tsp (2 mL) sea salt
½ cup (125 mL) extra virgin olive oil
1 bay leaf

You will want to use a pot with a tight-fitting lid. This recipe is a slow food classic, which is mostly why I think it belongs on a food truck. Don't be afraid to make a larger quantity and freeze the excess, which is what Erik does at his restaurant.

In a medium saucepan, melt butter over medium heat. Add onions and sweat for approximately 8 minutes, stirring occasionally. Add the tomatoes, salt, oil, and bay leaf. Cover with a lid, and reduce heat to low. Simmer for approximately 2 hours, stirring occasionally. If it is simmering too quickly, move pot off the centre of the burner to slow down the process.

Remove from heat, and empty contents into a blender or food processor. Blend until smooth.

NOTE *The large quantity of extra virgin olive oil tends to look a touch creamy after blending. Pass through a fine sieve if you have one, but it is not necessary. Set aside until ready to serve, or transfer to an airtight container and store in the refrigerator for up to 3 months.*

→ MAKES 4 CUPS (1 L) ←

Soups and CURRIES

Who doesn't like soup? I have a mean addiction for a tasty soup and a twitch for curries. I have fond memories from my childhood. My dad would make curry in a clay slow cooker, and he would place it in the oven overnight to cook. To let the flavours really meld together, the goal was to leave the curry in the refrigerator for five days before it was served. That curry would sit, covered, the pot glowing like the light of a lighthouse right at the back of the refrigerator. Woe betide me and my brother if we were caught sticking our fingers in that curry. Funny thing was, my dad was the worst for snacking on it. On many occasions I came into the kitchen to find him with the refrigerator door open, bent over, fork in hand, shoving curry down his gullet. Like a roo in headlights and with a mouthful of curry, he would say, "Quality control, sport". Like father like son, I raid my curry in the refrigerator all the time.

During the colder months, we serve a lot of soup and curry from the truck, and we are constantly changing the style and flavours. People have their favourites, but by far the most popular is the Tom Yum Soup (page 57). All summer people ask when the soup will be coming back, and I respond with, "When it gets cold!"

When making these soups and curries, I ask you to stick to the true amounts of chilies called for. The soups and curries that have a lot of spice are meant to be that way. If you make them without the true amount of chilies, you're not getting the

SOUPS

CURRIES

BUTTERNUT SQUASH AND RED CURRY SOUP

1 small butternut squash
1 cup (250 mL) coconut milk, divided
¼ cup (60 mL) Red Curry Paste (page 257)
¼ cup (60 mL) ground coriander
1 cup (250 mL) water
palm sugar, shaved, to taste
fish sauce, to taste
lime juice, to taste
¼ cup (60 mL) pine nuts
½ cup (125 mL) cilantro leaves
2 kaffir lime leaves, spines removed and
 finely julienned

This is a different take on the popular butternut squash soup. The ground coriander adds a robust earthiness and aromatic flavour to the sweetness of the squash, while the toasted pine nuts add crunch.

Preheat oven to 350°F (180°C).

Place pine nuts on a baking sheet in the oven, and toast until golden brown, 5 to 10 minutes. Remove from oven and allow to cool on the sheet to room temperature.

Peel the butternut squash, and cut in half lengthwise. Remove the seeds, and roughly chop the flesh into approximately ¾-inch (2 cm) cubes. Set aside at room temperature.

In a large pot, heat 1 Tbsp (15 mL) of coconut milk over high heat. Add Red Curry Paste, and fry for 2 minutes or until aromatic. Add coriander and cook for approximately 1 minute. Add squash, remaining coconut milk, and water. Stir to combine, cover with a lid, and bring to a simmer. Be careful not to boil. Cook for 15 minutes or until squash is tender and falling apart. Remove from heat.

Using an immersion blender, purée the mixture until smooth. Season with palm sugar, fish sauce, and lime juice.

Serve soup garnished with toasted pine nuts, cilantro, and kaffir lime leaves.

→→ SERVES 4 ←←

LAMB AND CLAM HARIRA

2 medium ripe tomatoes

2 Tbsp (30 mL) canola oil, divided

1 lb (500 g) lamb shoulder, cut into
    ½-inch (1 cm) cubes

8 clams

9 cups (2¼ L) water + water for tomatoes,
    divided (approx.)

1 small red onion, finely diced

3 cloves garlic, crushed

1 red bell pepper, diced

10 threads saffron

1 tsp (5 mL) ground ginger

1 tsp (5 mL) ground allspice

¼ tsp (1 mL) ground cinnamon

¼ tsp (1 mL) ground cardamom

1 tsp (5 mL) ground coriander

½ tsp (2 mL) ground cumin

½ cup (125 mL) dried chickpeas,
    soaked overnight

1 Tbsp (15 mL) Harissa (page 231)

1 Tbsp (15 mL) honey

juice of 2 lemons

kosher salt, to taste

black pepper, freshly cracked, to taste

½ cup (125 mL) cilantro leaves,
    finely chopped

Harira is a soup used by practising Muslims to break Ramadan. While travelling in Morocco, I prepared *harira* with the chef at one of the *riads* where I stayed; a *riad* is a traditional Moroccan house with an interior courtyard or garden. *Harira* is a vibrant, hearty soup that can be served as part of a meal or on its own as a light snack.

Fill a pot with water and bring to a boil over high heat. Remove the cores from tomatoes, and score the skin on the opposite end with a paring knife. Place the tomatoes in the boiling water, and count to 10. Turn off the heat, carefully remove tomatoes from water, and place in a sieve. Run the tomatoes under cold water until chilled, approximately 2 minutes. Peel the skin from the chilled tomatoes, and cut into quarters lengthwise. Remove the seeds, and finely dice the tomatoes. Set aside.

In a large, heavy-bottomed skillet, heat 1 Tbsp (15 mL) of oil over high heat. Place lamb in skillet, and cook for 5 minutes or until browned evenly. Remove lamb from skillet and place on paper towel to absorb excess liquid.

Submerge clams in cold water, and gently move clams around to remove as much sand and grit as possible. Remove clams from water, and place in a large stainless steel pot. Add 1 cup (250 mL) of water, cover with a lid, and bring to a boil over high heat. Reduce heat to medium-high, and simmer for 5 minutes or until it looks like all of the clams have opened. Discard any unopened clams. Remove from heat. Using tongs, carefully remove clams from pot and place in a container. Set aside in the refrigerator.

In a large stainless steel pot, heat 1 Tbsp (15 mL) of oil over high heat. Add onion and garlic and sweat, stirring occasionally, for 5 minutes or until translucent. Add pepper and prepared tomatoes, and sweat for approximately 3 minutes. Add saffron and spices, and cook for approximately 2 minutes, while stirring. Add soaked chickpeas, cooked lamb, and remaining 8 cups (2 L) of water. Bring to a boil and then reduce heat to medium. Simmer for 45 minutes or until chickpeas and lamb are tender.

 Add more water if needed, as the chickpeas will soak up liquid.

To serve, add cooked clams to the broth and warm for approximately 2 minutes. Season to taste with Harissa, honey, lemon juice, salt, and pepper. Add cilantro and stir to combine. Using a slotted spoon, equally portion the body of the soup across the serving bowls. Carefully ladle broth around the soup body in each bowl, and serve immediately.

Any remaining broth can be transferred to an airtight container and stored in the refrigerator for up to 5 days.

→ SERVES 4 WITH LEFTOVER BROTH ←

MISO SOUP WITH KANGAROO AND EGG NOODLES

2 cups (500 mL) dried egg noodles
1 Tbsp (15 mL) canola oil
1½ lb (750 g) kangaroo tenderloin
4 cups (1 L) Dashi (recipe follows)
½ cup (125 mL) white miso paste
2 small bok choy, roughly chopped
4 green onions, finely sliced

> White miso paste is prepared by fermenting soybeans with a specific fungus and grains. Prepared paste can be found at Asian grocers.

Kangaroo has steadily become a more mainstream protein in Australia, and is becoming more accessible in other parts of the world, including North America. It is an extremely lean meat, with a beautiful sweet flavour profile very similar to grass-fed beef. It is important to not overcook kangaroo meat because of its leanness. In this recipe, the kangaroo loins are quickly seared and then warmed by the miso broth. If you don't have access to kangaroo loin, you can substitute elk or venison for a similar but slightly more gamey protein.

Cook egg noodles according to package directions. Set aside at room temperature until ready to plate.

In a heavy-bottomed skillet, heat oil over high heat. Sear kangaroo for approximately 30 seconds on each side. Remove kangaroo from skillet and allow to rest at room temperature.

In a small pot, bring Dashi to a simmer over medium-high heat. Add miso paste, and stir to dissolve. Add bok choy, and remove from heat.

Slice seared kangaroo into ¼-inch (6 mm) thick slices.

To serve, place equal portions of sliced kangaroo and egg noodles into each serving bowl. Pour warm miso broth with bok choy over each bowl. Garnish with green onion and serve immediately.

→ SERVES 4 ←

DASHI

1 postcard-sized piece of kombu
4 cups (1 L) water
1 Tbsp (15 mL) dried bonito flakes

> Kombu is edible kelp, available at most Asian grocers.

In a large stainless steel pot, soak kombu in water for at least 30 minutes.

Place pot of kombu over medium heat, and allow to warm slowly. When the kombu begins to float, carefully remove it from the water and discard. Add bonito flakes, and increase heat to medium-high. Bring almost to a boil. Turn off heat, and let bonito flakes settle to the bottom of the pot.

Carefully strain the stock through a strainer lined with cheesecloth. Discard the bonito flakes and reserve the stock.

Use immediately or transfer to an airtight container and store in the refrigerator for up to 1 week.

→ MAKES 4 CUPS (1 L) ←

TOM KHA GAI SOUP

2 Tbsp (30 mL) + 1 tsp (5 mL) peanut
  oil, divided

2 stalks lemongrass, bruised and
  roughly sliced

6 kaffir lime leaves

3 cloves garlic, bruised

2-inches (5 cm) long piece ginger, peeled
  and roughly sliced

2-inches (5 cm) long piece galangal, peeled
  and roughly sliced

2 long red Thai chilies, pricked with a knife

1 red shallot, roughly sliced

3 cups (750 mL) coconut milk

4 boneless, skinless chicken thighs

1 cup (250 mL) enoki mushrooms

fish sauce, to taste

lime juice, to taste

palm sugar, shaved, to taste

½ cup (125 mL) cilantro leaves

Tom Kha Gai is a Thai lemongrass chicken soup. Heavy on the coconut, it is a sweeter, aromatic soup without the heat traditionally found in many other Thai soups. During the winter months, Tom Kha Gai is one of our most popular food-truck menu items, which we rotate frequently with other soups like Tom Yum.

In a pot, heat 2 Tbsp (30 mL) of oil over high heat. Add lemongrass, lime leaves, garlic, ginger, galangal, chilies, and shallot. Fry for 5 minutes or until fragrant. Add coconut milk and bring to a simmer. Do not boil. Once simmering, remove from heat and set aside to cool to room temperature and allow aromatics to infuse coconut milk.

When cool, strain the coconut milk mixture into another pot and discard the aromatics. Set aside at room temperature.

Cut chicken into ½-inch (1.5 cm) cubes, removing excess fat. In a frying pan, heat 1 tsp (5 mL) of oil over high heat. Sauté chicken for 5 minutes or until golden brown. Remove pan from heat and strain excess fat from chicken. Set aside at room temperature.

Bring the flavoured coconut milk back to a simmer over medium heat. Add cooked chicken and mushrooms, and simmer for approximately 1 minute. Remove from heat and add fish sauce, lime juice, and palm sugar.

NOTE *You should have a good balance of sweet, salty, and sour.*

Pour equal portions of soup into serving bowls. Garnish with cilantro and a squeeze of lime juice.

» SERVES 4 «

CLAM TOM YUM SOUP

10 dried red long Thai chilies, seeded

½ ripe pineapple, cored and roughly chopped

6 ripe Roma tomatoes, roughly chopped

6 shallots, roughly chopped

4 cloves garlic

3 green apples, roughly chopped

3 stalks lemongrass (white ends only), roughly chopped

8 kaffir lime leaves

½ cup (125 mL) cilantro roots

8 cups (2 L) water

24 clams

1 cup (250 mL) dried thick rice noodles

2 Tbsp (30 mL) Chili Jam (page 266)

palm sugar, shaved, to taste

fish sauce, to taste

1 cup (250 mL) bean sprouts

12 cherry tomatoes, halved lengthwise

½ cup (125 mL) cilantro leaves

3 cups (750 mL) Thai basil leaves

lime juice, to taste

> Tom yum broth must be made at least 1 day prior to serving.

Tom yum translates to "salad soup", and is easily one of Thailand's most popular soups. Traditionally, it is extremely spicy, and is the perfect lunch on a hot, humid day.

Soak chilies in warm water for 20 minutes to reconstitute. Remove from water and set aside at room temperature until ready to use.

In a food processor, combine pineapple, tomatoes, shallots, garlic, apples, lemongrass, lime leaves, cilantro roots, and soaked chilies. Purée until smooth.

Transfer contents into a large stainless steel pot and add the water. Bring to a boil over high heat, and then reduce heat to medium-high. Simmer for approximately 30 minutes, and then turn off heat. Cover the pot with a lid, and leave at room temperature for a minimum of 12 hours or overnight to allow the curry paste to steep.

Using the back of a ladle, and working in batches, push the soup liquid through a fine sieve into a clean pot, trying to yield as much broth as possible. Discard the paste left in the sieve. Broth can be used immediately or transferred to an airtight container and stored in the refrigerator for up to 1 week.

Submerge clams in cold water and gently move clams around to remove as much sand and grit as possible. Remove clams from water, and place in a large pot. Add 2 cups (500 mL) of Tom Yum broth to the pot, cover with a lid, and bring to a boil over high heat. Once boiling, reduce heat to medium-high, and simmer for 5 minutes or until it looks like all of the clams have opened. Discard any unopened clams. Remove from heat. Using tongs, carefully remove clams from pot, and set aside at room temperature.

Carefully pour as much clam broth as possible into another pot, being careful to leave behind any grit and sand from the clams. Discard leftover liquid and grit.

Soak rice noodles in about 4 cups (1 L) of boiling water for 5 minutes or until tender. Strain water and rinse noodles under cool running water to remove excess starch. Set rinsed noodles aside at room temperature.

Add Chili Jam and remaining original Tom Yum broth to the reserved clam Tom Yum broth, bring to a simmer over high heat, and then remove from heat. Season with palm sugar and fish sauce.

To serve, equally portion cooked rice noodles, bean sprouts, tomatoes, cilantro, basil, and clams into each soup bowl. Ladle 1 cup (250 mL) of clam Tom Yum broth over the ingredients in each bowl. Season with lime juice. Serve immediately.

Leftover broth can be stored in the refrigerator for up to 1 week.

→ SERVES 4 WITH LEFTOVER BROTH ←

CORN AND GREEN CURRY SOUP

1 Tbsp (15 mL) canola oil

⅓ cup (80 mL) Green Curry Paste
  (page 258)

kernels from 4 ears of corn

1 cup (250 mL) coconut milk

palm sugar, shaved, to taste

fish sauce, to taste

juice of 1 lime

8 sprigs cilantro

2 kaffir lime leaves, spines removed and
  finely julienned

In this soup, the flavour and sweetness of corn holds up very well to the intense aromatics of the Thai curry, and coconut milk adds a creamy texture reminiscent of traditional creamed corn.

In a large pot, heat oil over medium-high. Add Green Curry Paste, and cook for approximately 3 minutes to release aromas, stirring occasionally. Add corn, and sweat for approximately 4 minutes, while stirring. Add coconut milk, and stir to combine. Bring to a simmer, and then remove from heat.

Using an immersion blender, purée the corn mixture until smooth. Season with palm sugar, fish sauce, and lime juice.

Serve immediately garnished with torn cilantro and lime leaves.

↠ SERVES 4 ↞

POTATO AND LEEK SOUP WITH CANDIED BACON

1 leek (white part only)

¼ cup (60 mL) unsalted butter, divided

4 small Yukon gold potatoes,
  peeled and diced

4 cups (1 L) water

½ cup (125 mL) tarragon leaves

¼ cup (60 mL) sour cream

juice of 2 lemons

kosher salt, to taste

black pepper, freshly cracked, to taste

¼ cup (60 mL) chopped Candied Bacon
  (page 249)

The addition of tarragon to this popular soup adds a subtle anise flavour that rounds out the buttery richness of the soup body. Candied bacon adds a decadent, sweet, and salty treat to the bowl. This soup makes for a hearty, belly-warming bowl served street-side during the colder months.

Remove root base from leek and discard. Cut leek in half lengthwise, and then slice crosswise into ¼-inch (6 mm) thick slices. Place leek slices in a basin of cold water and move around to release any grit and sand. Allow sediment to sink to the bottom of the basin, and carefully transfer leeks into a colander to drain.

In a large stainless steel pot, melt half of the butter over medium-high heat. Increase heat to high, and add leeks. Reduce heat to medium-low, and sweat leeks for approximately 5 minutes, while stirring. Remove leeks from pot, and set aside at room temperature.

In the pot used for sweating the leeks, add potatoes, remaining butter, and water. Bring to a simmer over medium-high heat, and cook for 15 minutes or until potatoes start falling apart. Using an immersion blender, purée potatoes in the water until smooth. Return leeks to the pot along with tarragon leaves and sour cream. Stir to combine. Season with lemon juice, salt, and pepper.

To serve, garnish soup with Candied Bacon. Serve immediately.

» SERVES 4 «

BEET BORSCHT WITH DILL SOUR CREAM

1 cup (250 mL) dill fronds, divided

½ cup (125 mL) sour cream

1 Tbsp (15 mL) canola oil

1 medium yellow onion, diced

4 red beets, peeled and diced

1 cup (250 mL) prepared sauerkraut

1 cup (250 mL) vodka

juice of 2 lemons

kosher salt, to taste

black pepper, freshly cracked, to taste

Sauerkraut translates to "sour cabbage"; it is made by layering finely sliced cabbage with salt and allowing it to ferment. It is popular worldwide, and is a common hot dog condiment at street-side stands and baseball games in North America.

Borscht is a simple soup with many variations and styles. As with any dish that focusses on one main ingredient, the key is in perfecting the flavour and balance of the dish.

Finely chop half of the dill and place in a small bowl. Add sour cream, and stir well to combine. Set aside in the refrigerator.

In a large pot, heat oil over high heat. Reduce heat to medium-low, add onions, and sweat for 5 minutes or until translucent. Add beets, sauerkraut, and vodka. Increase heat to medium-high, bring mixture to a simmer, and cook until beets are tender and falling apart. Remove from heat. Add remaining dill and purée with an immersion blender until smooth. Add lemon juice, and season with salt and pepper.

Ladle soup into serving bowls, and spoon equal portions of dill sour cream onto the centre of each soup. Serve immediately.

→→ SERVES 4 ←←

RED CURRY BEEF CHEEK WITH GREEN BEAN SALAD

12 cups (3 L) Master Stock (page 263)

2 Tbsp (30 mL) grape seed oil

2 beef cheeks, cleaned and trimmed

1 batch Coconut Red Curry
  (recipe follows)

1 Tbsp (15 mL) peanut oil

40 green beans (approx.)

½ cup (125 mL) Chili Caramel (page 265)

1 batch Herb Salad (recipe follows)

1 lime, quartered

> To save time, you can ask your butcher to clean the raw beef cheeks when you buy them, removing sinew, excess fat, and skin.

This is a beautifully bold dish with huge flavours that meld together well. The creamy aromatic red curry sauce cuts through the richness of beef cheeks, while the crispness of the beans and herb salad add a crunchy texture and fresh lift to the dish. I prefer to use beef cheek over other cuts of beef as a braising meat because it holds up well to longer cooking, has a great flavour and texture, and won't dry out.

In a stock pot, bring Master Stock to a simmer over medium-high heat.

Cut beef cheeks into four equal portions. Set aside at room temperature while you heat oil.

While stock is coming to a simmer, heat grape seed oil in a frying pan over high heat. Sear beef cheeks for 10 minutes total, or until golden brown on all sides. Remove beef cheeks from pan and place into the simmering Master Stock. Cover pot with lid, and braise beef cheeks for 1.5 hours or until tender and on the verge of falling apart. Remove stock from heat and set aside.

Prepare Coconut Red Curry and Herb Salad according to recipes that follow.

Once Coconut Red Curry is prepared, use a slotted spoon to carefully transfer beef cheeks from Master Stock to pot of Coconut Red Curry. Allow Master Stock to cool to room temperature, then store in an airtight container in the refrigerator or freezer until next use.

In a wok, heat peanut oil over high heat until it starts to smoke. Add green beans and toss for 3 minutes, allowing beans to become slightly scorched. Transfer beans to a bowl and dress liberally with Chili Caramel.

Place dressed beans on the centre of a serving plate. Top with cooked beef cheeks and Coconut Red Curry. Place Herb Salad on top, and serve with wedges of lime.

→ SERVES 4 ←

COCONUT RED CURRY SAUCE

1 cup (250 mL) coconut milk, divided
½ cup (125 mL) Red Curry Paste
  (page 257)
palm sugar, shaved, to taste
fish sauce, to taste
lime juice, to taste

In a wok, scorch ¼ cup (60 mL) of coconut milk over high heat for 3 minutes or until it separates and becomes oily and shiny. Be careful not to let the coconut milk burn. Add Red Curry Paste and fry for 2 minutes or until aromatic. Add remaining coconut milk and bring to a simmer over medium heat for approximately 3 minutes. Do not boil. Season with palm sugar, fish sauce, and lime juice. Set aside.

→ MAKES 1 ¼ CUPS (310 ML) ←

HERB SALAD

¾-inch (2 cm) long piece lemongrass
  (white end only)
4 sprigs cilantro, picked
4 sprigs Thai basil, picked
4 sprigs mint, picked
¾-inch (2 cm) long piece ginger, peeled
  and finely julienned
bird's eye chilies, finely
  julienned, to taste
1 small red shallot, finely sliced into rings
lime juice, to taste

Using a sharp knife, finely slice lemongrass on an angle. Place all ingredients, except the lime juice, in a bowl. Dress with lime juice and toss gently to combine. Set aside.

→ SERVES 4 ←

RENDANG CURRY OF BEEF CHEEK

1 Tbsp (15 mL) canola oil

2 beef cheeks, cleaned, trimmed, and cut into
  1¼-inches (3 cm) cubes

1 cup (250 mL) coconut milk, divided

1 cup (250 mL) Rendang Curry Paste
  (page 257)

3 Tbsp (45 mL) tamarind water

palm sugar, shaved, to taste

fish sauce, to taste

lime juice, to taste

¼ cup (60 mL) Fried Shallots (page 250)

1 cup (250 mL) cilantro leaves

2 kaffir lime leaves, spines remove and
  finely julienned

> To save time, you can ask your butcher to clean the raw beef cheeks when you buy them.

Rendang curry originates from Indonesia, but it is also commonly eaten on the streets of Malaysia and surrounding Southeast Asian countries. In Indonesia, *rendang* curries are traditionally served during celebrations like weddings and other ceremonial feasts. After braising, beef cheeks are very similar in mouth feel to shank meat, with a sticky and gelatinous texture.

In a large, heavy-bottomed pot, heat oil over high heat. Place beef cheeks in the pot and cook for 5 minutes or until browned evenly on all sides. Cover browned beef cheeks with water. Bring to a boil over high heat, and then reduce heat to medium-high and bring to a simmer. Simmer for 45 minutes or until beef is tender. With a slotted spoon, remove cheeks from water and set aside at room temperature.

Discard braising liquid from the pot, add 2 Tbsp (30 mL) of coconut milk, and heat over high heat. Add Rendang Curry Paste, and cook for 3 minutes or until aromatic. Add tamarind water and remaining coconut milk. Stir to combine. Add cooked beef cheeks, and bring to a simmer without boiling. Season with palm sugar, fish sauce, and lime juice.

To serve, place equal portions of curry in each serving bowl. Garnish with Fried Shallots, cilantro, and lime leaves. Serve immediately.

➔ SERVES 4 ⬅

BUTTER CHICKEN WITH ROTI

SAUCE

6 red shallots, roughly chopped

4 cloves garlic

2 ⅓-inches (6 cm) long piece ginger, peeled and roughly chopped

6 dried, bird's eye chilies, seeded

2 stalks lemongrass (white ends only), finely chopped

4 medium very ripe tomatoes, seeded

¼ cup (60 mL) tomato paste

1 tsp (5 mL) ground turmeric

1 tsp (5 mL) paprika

1 tsp (5 mL) ground cinnamon

1 tsp (5 mL) ground coriander

1 tsp (5 mL) ground cumin

½ tsp (2 mL) ground cardamom

¼ tsp (1 mL) ground cloves

½ tsp (2 mL) ground nutmeg

½ tsp (2 mL) ground mace

BUTTER CHICKEN

8 boneless, skinless chicken thighs, fat trimmed

1 Tbsp (15 mL) canola oil

½ cup (125 mL) unsalted butter

2 cups (500 mL) full-fat yogurt

palm sugar, shaved, to taste

fish sauce, to taste

juice of 3 lemons

4 roti

Butter chicken is a dish that everyone loves. When the effort is made to prepare this dish properly, the end product is worth all of the work. During the colder months in Canada, butter chicken is an ideal street-food meal that warms your belly on a cold day. Roti, found at most Asian and Caribbean grocers, is the perfect street-food scoop to soak up this saucy dish.

TO MAKE THE SAUCE, in a food processor, purée all of the ingredients until smooth. Set aside at room temperature.

Cut each chicken thigh into 4 to 6 equal-sized pieces.

Soak chilies in warm water for 20 minutes to reconstitute. Remove from water and set aside at room temperature until ready to use.

In a heavy-bottomed skillet, heat oil over high heat. Place chicken in the skillet, and cook for 5 minutes or until evenly browned. Remove from heat, and strain excess fat from chicken. Set aside at room temperature.

In a large stainless steel pot, melt butter over medium-high heat. Add the blender contents to the butter, cooking over high heat, while stirring, for 5 minutes or until aromatic. Add browned chicken and yogurt, stirring to combine. Simmer for approximately 5 minutes, being careful not to boil. Season with palm sugar, fish sauce, and lemon juice.

Serve immediately with warmed roti.

» SERVES 4 «

Both mace and nutmeg, though similar in flavour, are used in the sauce recipe. Mace adds a bright orange hue, like saffron, contributing to butter chicken's recognizable colour.

GREEN CURRY CHICKEN AND MUSSELS

4 boneless, skinless chicken thighs,
  fat trimmed

1 Tbsp canola or sunflower oil

1 cup (250 mL) coconut milk, divided

1 cup (250 mL) Green Curry Paste
  (page 258)

24 large fresh mussels

palm sugar, shaved, to taste

fish sauce, to taste

lime juice, to taste

3 cups (750 mL) Thai basil leaves

The sweet, earthy flavour of mussels enhances chicken when served together. The intense heat and flavour of green curry is perfect with mussels and chicken, as both proteins stand up to the full flavour.

Cut each chicken thigh into 4 to 6 equal-sized pieces.

In a heavy-bottomed skillet, heat oil over high heat. Place chicken in the skillet, and cook for 5 minutes or until evenly browned. Remove from heat, and drain excess fat from chicken. Set aside at room temperature.

In a large pot, heat 1 Tbsp (15 mL) of coconut milk and all of the Green Curry Paste over high heat. Fry for 3 minutes or until aromatic. Add remaining coconut milk, and stir well to combine. Add cooked chicken and mussels, cover with a lid, and bring to a simmer. Be careful not to boil. Cook for 5 minutes or until it looks like all mussels have opened. Discard any unopened mussels.

Season curry with palm sugar, fish sauce, and lime juice. Garnish with basil, and serve immediately.

→ SERVES 4 ←

When it comes to protein, I lean towards fish and seafood more than land meats for eating and cooking. That being said, I have a real soft spot for lamb and pork. There's nothing quite like the sweet, succulent flavour of a spring lamb or the rich fattiness of a well-raised pig. Both meats have a multitude of potential uses, and both hold up well to a myriad of flavour marriages. Since coming to Canada, where lamb isn't as popular or as accessible as it is in Australia, I have adapted some of my favourite recipes to use a variety of beef cuts. I am also a massive fan of beef tartare, and the two recipes here are not your normal take on this classic dish.

BEEF

BEEF TARTARE WITH SMOKED
TOMATO AIOLI **71**

AUSSIE BURGER WITH THE LOT **73**

BIERE DE GARDE BULL-BOAR BAO **74**

BRAISED BEEF CHEEK WITH PRESERVED
FRENCH BEANS **76**

COLD-SMOKED SWEETBREADS WITH
CELERIAC PURÉE **78**

BRAISED BEEF WITH CINNAMON
AND ANISE **80**

STIR-FRIED BEEF AND SNAKE
BEANS **81**

SOUTHERN SMOKED BEEF BRISKET
SANDWICH **82**

VIETNAMESE MARINATED BEEF
SALAD **84**

RAS EL HANOUT BEEF SKEWERS **86**

GAME

SEARED VENISON WITH CORN
FRITTERS AND CHERRY
GASTRIQUE **87**

VENISON SAUSAGES WITH GARLICKY
KALE **89**

LAMB

LAMB SOUVLAKI **91**

LAMB LADY'S FINGERS **92**

LAMB TARTARE WITH CHERMOULA **94**

LAMB SKEWERS WITH TOUM **96**

KOFTA AND EGG TAGINE **97**

PORK

CRISPY PIG TONGUES WITH PICKLED
FENNEL **99**

BABI IN A BOWL **101**

MASTER STOCK BRAISED PORK BELLY
WITH GREEN PAPAYA SALAD **102**

MASTER STOCK BRAISED PORK HOCK
BAO **108**

POULTRY

CHICKEN POT STICKERS **110**

CHICKEN SATAY SKEWERS **114**

CRISPY SKIN DUCK WITH SPRING
ONION PANCAKES **115**

FOIE GRAS AND GNOCCHI POUTINE **116**

FRIED CHICKEN AND CANDIED BACON
WAFFLES **119**

RAS EL HANOUT BRAISED CHICKEN
WITH FRAGRANT COUSCOUS **120**

BEEF TARTARE WITH SMOKED TOMATO AIOLI

¼ baguette, finely sliced crosswise

⅓ cup (80 mL) (approx.) + 1 Tbsp (15 mL) sunflower oil

kosher salt, to taste

black pepper, freshly cracked, to taste

1 lb (500 g) beef tenderloin

2 small red shallots, finely diced

1 Tbsp (15 mL) capers, finely chopped

3 Tbsp (45 mL) cornichons, finely chopped

1 egg yolk

2 Tbsp (30 mL) parmesan cheese, finely grated

½ cup (125 mL) cilantro leaves, finely chopped

½ cup (125 mL) flat leaf parsley leaves, finely chopped

1 Tbsp (15 mL) chives, finely sliced

1 Tbsp (15 mL) Fried Shallots (page 250)

1 Tbsp (15 mL) Fried Garlic (page 251)

½ cup (125 mL) Smoked Tomato Aioli (page 272)

This recipe is one of my takes on a classic beef tartare. To complement classic tartare ingredients like parmesan, cornichons, and capers, this tartare is served with smoked tomato aioli. The heat and smokiness of the aioli creates a barbeque flavour experience.

Preheat oven to 250°F (120°C).

Make crostini by spreading baguette slices on a baking sheet, and sprinkle the surface of the slices with up to ⅓ cup (80 mL) of oil, using only as much as needed. Season with salt and pepper, and place in the oven. Bake for 12 to 15 minutes or until lightly golden. Remove from oven and set aside at room temperature.

Place a very clean cutting board in the refrigerator, and allow to cool for approximately 10 minutes.

While the cutting board is chilling, place 2 handfuls of ice in a medium bowl. Nestle a smaller bowl into the ice, and place bowls in the refrigerator.

Return the chilled cutting board to your work surface. Wearing gloves and using a very sharp knife, finely slice the beef into disks crosswise. Finely dice the sliced beef, and transfer into the chilled bowl.

Add the shallots, capers, cornichons, egg yolk, parmesan, chopped herbs (excluding the chives) and 1 Tbsp (15 mL) of oil to the beef. Using a very clean stainless steel spoon, mix to combine thoroughly. Season with salt and pepper.

To serve, spoon equal portions of tartare in the centre of each serving plate. Using the back of a large spoon, press down on the centre of the tartare to create a flat, wide surface. Sprinkle the entire surface of the tartare with the chives, Fried Shallots, and Fried Garlic. Place a small spoonful of Smoked Tomato Aioli in the centre of the tartare. Serve immediately with crostini.

» SERVES 4 «

AUSSIE BURGER WITH THE LOT

¾ lb (375 g) beef chuck (approx.)

1 small carrot, finely grated

2 red shallots, finely diced

2 cloves garlic, finely chopped

½ cup (125 mL) flat leaf parsley leaves, finely chopped

kosher salt, to taste

black pepper, freshly cracked, to taste

1 Tbsp (15 mL) canola oil

1 yellow onion, finely sliced

4 slices thick-cut double-smoked bacon

4 thick pineapple rings, each approx. ¼ inch (6 mm) thick

1 Tbsp (15 mL) olive oil

2 Tbsp (30 mL) unsalted butter

4 eggs

4 slices Australian or aged Canadian cheddar

4 burger buns

8 slices pickled beets

4 leaves iceberg lettuce

4 slices tomato

ketchup, to taste

> Thick-cut double-smoked bacon is available at butchers or specialty delicatessens.

In Australia, fish and chip shops are as popular for their fish and chips as they are for their made-to-order burgers. I would go to my local fish and chip shop to get what is called a "burger with the lot". I would stand in line behind a few tradies—construction workers, electricians, plumbers, and the like, waiting to get their lunchtime feed—watching the cook behind the counter grilling burgers like they were going out of fashion. The egg would be perfectly fried, crispy on the bottom and yolk ready to burst.

In order to eat these beasts, I would have to sit on a park bench surrounded by hundreds of hungry seagulls. Legs spread, elbows on my knees so as not to end up with a lap of egg yolk, beet juice, and whatever else wants to pour out from my giant burger. I would wash it all down with iced coffee.

Using a meat grinder, grind the beef chuck and place meat in a bowl. Add carrot, shallots, garlic, parsley, salt, and pepper. Wearing gloves, mix well to combine. Form equally portioned patties, and set aside in the refrigerator.

Preheat grill or barbecue to highest temperature.

In a skillet, heat canola oil over high heat. Place onions in skillet, and fry for 4 to 5 minutes or until onions are scorched and tender. Remove from heat and set aside.

Place burgers, bacon slices, and pineapple on the barbecue.

While the burgers are grilling, heat olive oil and butter in a clean skillet over high heat. Without breaking the yolks, fry the eggs sunny side up for 4 minutes or until the egg whites are crispy and the yolks are still runny. Carefully place fried onions and bacon on the yolks. Remove from heat and set aside at room temperature, if eggs are done before burgers.

After you've grilled one side of the burgers, flip them over and place the cheddar on top of the patties. Nestle the grilled pineapple into the melting cheese. Cook burgers for 3 minutes or until medium-rare. Remove burgers from grill.

To serve, build burgers by placing the burger on the bottom bun, followed by the fried egg with onion and bacon, pickled beet slices, lettuce, tomato, ketchup (known in Australia as "tomato sauce"), and the top bun. Serve immediately with a cold beer or an iced coffee.

→ SERVES 4 ←

BIERE DE GARDE BULL-BOAR BAO

½ lb (250 g) pork shoulder, trimmed,
  finely ground
½ lb (250 g) beef chuck, trimmed,
  finely ground
8 cloves garlic, minced
2 Tbsp (30 mL) kosher salt (approx.)
1 tsp (5 mL) ground allspice
1 tsp (5 mL) ground coriander seeds
1 tsp (5 mL) freshly cracked black pepper
1 tsp (5 mL) ground anise
½ tsp (2 mL) ground nutmeg
½ tsp (2 mL) ground fennel seeds
¼ tsp (1 mL) ground cardamom
¾ cup (185 mL) red wine (preferably Shiraz)
¾ cup (185 mL) Niagara Oast House
  Brewers Biere de Garde or a similar
  Belgian-style beer
8 Steamed Buns (page 255)
16 slices prepared pickled beets
1 batch Zhoug (page 274)

The original bull-boar sausage recipe comes from Central Victoria, Australia, where Swiss-Italian immigrants settled in the 1850s and '60s. A small group of families guarded their recipes for the bull-boar sausage and handed them down through the generations. The specifics of the original recipes have always been kept top secret, but it is generally known that they include beef, pork, garlic, spices, and red wine. To prevent the original recipes from being lost forever, the bull-boar sausage is on the endangered recipe list curated by the slow food movement. The following recipe is my attempt to get as close to the flavour profile of the sausages that I got from my favourite butcher in Newstead, Victoria, Australia. This recipe is for patties, but feel free to make sausages from the mixture. This recipe uses Niagara Oast House Brewers' Biere de Garde, which adds subtle malt-driven chocolate and cherry flavours and a spicy raw cocoa bean finish. It is the perfect addition for a sausage mixture that is seasoned with Christmastime spices like nutmeg and cardamom.

Wearing kitchen gloves, combine all ingredients except Steamed Buns, pickled beets, and Zhoug in a large stainless steel bowl. Transfer to a resealable bag, and place in the refrigerator for 4 to 5 days to marinate. The liquids will be absorbed by the meat while it marinates.

On the cooking day, prepare Steamed Buns and time the preparation so that buns are freshly steamed as close to the serving time as possible.

When ready to cook, form meat mixture into 8 equal patties.

Heat the barbecue or indoor grill to highest setting.

Grill patties for 5 minutes total or until both sides are slightly charred and the meat is cooked through. Remove from grill, and set aside at room temperature.

Open Steamed Buns and place one patty in each. Garnish with pickled beets and Zhoug. Serve immediately.

➤ SERVES 4 ◄

BRAISED BEEF CHEEK WITH PRESERVED FRENCH BEANS

RECIPE BY GUEST CHEF: NATHAN YOUNG, RAVINE VINEYARD ESTATE WINERY RESTAURANT, ST. DAVID'S ONTARIO

1 head celeriac, cut into ¾-inch (2 cm) dice

2 cups (500 mL) whole milk (approx.) (enough to cover half of the celeriac)

2 cups (500 mL) chicken stock (approx.) (enough to cover half of the celeriac)

1 Tbsp (15 mL) grape seed oil

4 beef cheeks, cleaned and trimmed

3 cups (750 mL) red wine

2 large yellow onions, quartered

2 carrots, quartered lengthwise

6 stalks celery, cut into 2-inch (5 cm) pieces

½ cup (125 mL) thyme leaves

1 tsp (5 mL) whole black peppercorns

5 bay leaves

4 cups (1 L) beef broth

2 tsp (10 mL) kosher salt

½ cup (125 mL) unsalted butter

4 cups (1 L) pickled green beans

½ tsp (2 mL) olive oil

> You can ask your butcher to clean the beef cheeks for you when you buy them.

Nathan Young is an exceptional talent that the Niagara region is lucky to have. He has a true passion for food and cooking, and is a real gentleman. I look forward to collaborating with him regularly and seeing what we can come up with together. In this recipe, Nate uses Wachs Farms pickled green beans from Ravine Vineyard, which are grown on the vineyard property and pickled in-house. Your favourite brand of pickled beans can be used as a substitute.

When I asked Nate what he would serve on a food truck, he told me about this dish, which we both agreed would be perfect to serve street-side on a cold day.

Preheat oven to 325°F (165°C).

In a small saucepan, cover celeriac with milk and chicken stock. Set aside at room temperature.

In a heavy-bottomed skillet, heat grape seed oil over medium heat. Sear beef cheeks for 5 minutes or until all sides are golden brown. Remove cheeks from skillet and pat dry with a paper towel to remove excess fat.

Place cheeks in an oven-safe Dutch oven, and add wine, onion, carrot, celery, thyme, peppercorns, bay leaves, and beef broth. Braise in the oven, uncovered, for approximately 1½ hours. Remove from oven, flip the beef cheeks over, cover with a lid, and return to oven for an additional 1½ hours or until fork-tender and they break apart slightly at the touch of a finger.

While the beef cheeks are braising, add salt and butter to the celeriac. Cook over medium-high heat for 15 minutes or until celeriac is fork-tender. Strain, reserving the liquid in pan. Transfer celeriac to a food processor.

Bring reserved cooking liquid to a boil over high heat, and remove from heat. Slowly and carefully add hot liquid to the food processor as you purée the celeriac until the mixture reaches the consistency of a soft mashed potato. The remaining liquid can be reserved for a homemade soup base.

Remove cheeks from Dutch oven; strain the braising liquid into a clean saucepan through a fine sieve. Strain the liquid, discarding any remaining solids. Place the saucepan over medium heat, and cook for 30 minutes or until the liquid has reduced by half of its volume.

Strain green beans through a colander, and add to a pan over medium heat with olive oil. Sauté for 2 minutes or until warmed through. Keep warm until ready to plate meal.

To serve, use a large serving spoon to place celeriac purée in the centre of each serving plate. Add approximately 9 sautéed beans beside the purée, and place a beef cheek next to the purée. Ladle approximately ¼ cup (60 mL) of braise reduction directly over the beef cheek. Serve immediately.

→ SERVES 4 ←

COLD-SMOKED SWEETBREADS WITH CELERIAC PURÉE

RECIPE BY GUEST CHEF: ANDREW MCLEOD, ST. CATHARINES, ONTARIO

1 lb (500 g) veal sweetbreads

2 cups (500 mL) buttermilk

¼ cup (60 mL) kosher salt

¼ cup (60 mL) thyme leaves, divided

4 cloves garlic, finely sliced, divided

6 whole black peppercorns, cracked

4 large eggs

2 cups (500 mL) panko bread crumbs

2 cups (500 mL) all-purpose flour

4 cups (1 L) + 1 Tbsp (15 mL) canola oil

1 batch Celeriac Purée (recipe follows)

1 cup (250 mL) radicchio, julienned

1 Tbsp (15 mL) toasted walnuts, crushed

kosher salt, to taste

black pepper, freshly cracked, to taste

> You will need a cold smoker and 2 cups (500 mL) of hickory wood chips. Alternatively, you can use a barbeque set up for indirect smoking.

Andrew McLeod has shown our business a huge amount of support, and has become a great personal friend since we met during our first summer operating the food truck. We have bonded very well and feed off of each other's passion for food and cooking, usually over a lot of wine. Andrew is very talented, with an exceptional skill and palate.

This dish takes a total of 2 days to prepare, but it is worth every minute. Because the majority of the work is done ahead of time, it is a great dish for entertaining at home or for street-food service.

Cover sweetbreads in cold water, and place in the refrigerator to soak for 24 hours, changing water every 5 hours, if possible.

For the brine, combine buttermilk, kosher salt, half of the thyme, 2 cloves of garlic, and peppercorns in a bowl. Mix to combine, and set aside at room temperature.

Strain water from sweetbreads and cover with brine. Soak in the refrigerator for a further 24 hours.

Remove sweetbreads from brine and pat dry with paper towel. Using your thumb and forefinger, carefully peel the thin membrane from the outside of the sweetbreads and discard. Set sweetbreads aside in the refrigerator.

If you are using a cold smoker, set up the wood chips and smoker according to manufacturer's directions. If you don't have access to a cold smoker, set up a smoke pouch by placing a 50/50 mixture of wet and dry wood chips in foil. Fold to close all edges of the foil tightly. Puncture bag with a fork on one side only. Preheat barbecue to high. Place bag over the flames and heat until wood chips are smoking. Reduce heat to lowest possible setting and allow heat to escape the barbecue by opening the lid for 5 minutes. Place sweetbreads on the barbecue, close the lid, and smoke for 4 hours.

Once smoked, remove sweetbreads from the smoker and allow to cool to room temperature. Transfer to the refrigerator to cool completely.

Once chilled, portion sweetbreads into roughly 1 oz (30 mL) pieces. Don't worry about the pieces being perfectly even in size.

Crack eggs into a small bowl and whisk well.

In a separate a small bowl, combine remaining thyme and panko. Set up a crumbing station, with flour, eggs, and thyme-panko each in separate bowls, in that order.

Crumb sweetbreads by lightly coating in flour then soaking in eggs for approximately 30 seconds. Transfer sweetbreads to panko bowl. Toss to coat well. Place on a tray and repeat this process until all sweetbreads are crumbed. Set aside in the refrigerator.

In a large, heavy-bottomed pot, heat 4 cups (1 L) of canola oil to 350°F (180°C).

Working in batches of 3 or 4 at a time, carefully lower crumbed sweetbread into hot oil and deep-fry for 3 to 4 minutes or until crispy and golden brown. Using a spider or slotted spoon, carefully transfer sweetbreads to paper towel to absorb excess oil. Repeat this process until all sweetbreads are cooked.

While you are frying the sweetbreads, gently warm the Celeriac Purée over low heat for approximately 4 minutes.

In a wok or heavy-bottomed skillet, stir-fry the radicchio and remaining garlic slices in 1 Tbsp (15 mL) of oil over high heat for 3 to 4 minutes or until radicchio is softened. Remove from heat, and add walnuts. Stir to combine, and season with salt and pepper.

To serve, place ¼ cup (60 mL) portions of Celeriac Purée in the middle of each plate and top with equal portions of radicchio. Place crispy sweetbreads on top of the radicchio, and garnish with your favourite baby herbs.

→→ SERVES 4 ←←

CELERIAC PURÉE

1 large celeriac, roughly cubed
3 Tbsp (45 mL) unsalted butter
4 sprigs thyme
1 cup (250 mL) buttermilk
kosher salt, to taste

In a small pot, combine celeriac, butter, thyme, and buttermilk. Bring to a simmer over medium heat. Once simmering, reduce heat to medium-low and gently cook for 15 minutes or until the celeriac is falling apart. Remove from heat and allow to cool slightly. Discard thyme sprigs.

Transfer mixture to a blender, and purée until very smooth. Transfer to a clean small pot, season with salt, and set aside until ready to serve.

→→ MAKES 3 CUPS (750 ML) ←←

BRAISED BEEF WITH CINNAMON AND ANISE

3 red long Thai chilies

8 cups (2 L) Veal Stock (page 264)

2 sticks cinnamon

6 whole star anise

2 stalks lemongrass (white parts only)

2⅓-inches (6 cm) long piece ginger, peeled
  and roughly chopped

6 red shallots, quartered

4 kaffir lime leaves

4 cloves garlic

1 Tbsp (15 mL) canola oil

2 beef shanks

4 chicken or duck eggs

2 cups (500 mL) jasmine rice

1 cup (250 mL) Thai basil leaves

1 cup (250 mL) cilantro leaves

1 lime, quartered

¼ cup (60 mL) Chili Caramel (page 265)

This dish is inspired by one of my favourite daily street-food meals in Bangkok. Using star anise in the braising enhances the beef flavour, while the cinnamon adds an aromatic sweetness. The hard-boiled egg also absorbs the flavours and colours of the braising stock, and provides a nice contrast in texture to the beef.

Prick chilies with a knife. In a large pot, combine Veal Stock, cinnamon, star anise, lemongrass, ginger, shallots, lime leaves, garlic, and chilies. Bring to a simmer over high heat. Once stock reaches a simmer, turn off heat and leave the pot on the burner.

While bringing the stock to a simmer, heat oil in a large, heavy-bottomed skillet over high heat. Cook beef shanks for 5 minutes or until evenly browned on all sides.

Transfer the browned shanks to the stock, and return stock to a simmer over high heat. Braise shanks, uncovered, at a simmer, for 2 hours or until the shank meat is falling off the bone. Approximately 10 minutes before the beef is done cooking, place the eggs, in their shells, into the stock. Cook for 10 minutes.

Using a spider or slotted spoon, carefully remove hard-boiled eggs and beef shanks from the broth. Place shanks on a tray, and set aside at room temperature. Place eggs on a separate tray, and peel. Strain remaining stock through a chinois or fine strainer into a smaller pot. Discard the aromatic ingredients.

Pick shank meat from the bones, and transfer the meat back to the stock with the peeled eggs. Set aside at room temperature.

Prepare jasmine rice in a rice cooker according to the manufacturer's directions.

To serve, bring the stock with beef and eggs back to a simmer over medium heat. Once simmering, remove from heat.

Place equal portions of rice into each serving bowl. Using the back of a spoon, create a dimple in the centre of the rice. Remove the peeled eggs from the stock, and cut them in half, lengthwise. Set aside. Place equal portions of meat in the dimple of the rice. Spoon approximately ¼ cup (60 mL) of stock into each serving bowl.

Place two egg halves into each serving bowl. Garnish with basil and cilantro. Serve immediately with lime wedges and Chili Caramel on the side.

→ SERVES 4 ←

STIR-FRIED BEEF AND SNAKE BEANS

¾ lb (375 g) beef tenderloin

2 cups (500 mL) jasmine rice

2 Tbsp (30 mL) + 1 Tbsp (15 mL) canola oil

4 eggs

24 snake beans (Chinese long
  beans), quartered

½ cup (125 mL) Chili Jam (page 266)

12 dried bird's eye chilies, seeded

4 fresh bird's eye chilies, seeded and
  quartered lengthwise

1 cup (250 mL) Thai basil leaves

¼ cup (60 mL) Chili Caramel (page 265)

1 lime, quartered

I ate this stir-fry frequently for breakfast in Thailand, and it was a great way to wake up in the morning. With both dried and fresh bird's eye chilies, this dish is ridiculously spicy and gets your endorphins flowing to kick-start the day.

Soak dried chilies in warm water for 20 minutes. Remove chilies and cut into thirds, crosswise. Set aside at room temperature.

Using a sharp knife, cut the beef across the grain into ¼-inch (6 mm) thick slices. Then cut each slice into ¼-inch (6 mm) wide strips. Set aside in the refrigerator.

Cook rice in a rice cooker according to manufacturer's directions. Set aside, keeping warm.

Time the cooking process so that the beef and the eggs are finished cooking at the same time. Heat a wok and a non-stick or cast iron skillet over high heat. Add 2 Tbsp (30 mL) of oil to the wok, and 1 Tbsp (15 mL) of oil to the skillet. Crack the eggs into the skillet, being sure not to break the yolks. Reduce heat to medium-low for the skillet. Add the beef slices and snake beans to the wok. Stir-fry for approximately 2 minutes. Add Chili Jam to the wok along with dried and fresh chilies. Toss to combine. Add the basil, and toss to combine. Remove the wok from heat. At this point, the egg whites should have charred slightly. The yolk should still be runny. Remove eggs from heat.

To serve, spoon equal portions of rice into each serving bowl. Place stir-fried beef on top of rice, and fried egg on top of stir-fried beef. Serve with Chili Caramel and lime wedges on the side.

→→ SERVES 4 ←←

SOUTHERN SMOKED BEEF BRISKET SANDWICH

RECIPE BY GUEST CHEF: TREVOR JANISSE, PERSONAL CHEF AT FOOD TROUBADOUR, STONEY CREEK, ONTARIO

BARBECUE RUB

1 Tbsp (15 mL) kosher salt

1 Tbsp (15 mL) cracked black pepper

1 Tbsp (15 mL) paprika

1 Tbsp (15 mL) ground cumin

1 Tbsp (15 mL) dry mustard powder

2 cups (500 mL) Barbecue Sauce
  (recipe follows), divided

4.4 lb (2 kg) beef brisket, with fat cap

2 cups (500 mL) water

dash of Worcestershire sauce

Hickory wood chips

Slaw (recipe follows)

4 egg buns

> This recipe requires a hot smoker to achieve a consistent temperature and smoking throughout the brisket-smoking process. Barbeques are unreliable in this respect, and thus are not a good substitute for smoking the brisket. Make sure you select a brisket that has a somewhat consistent thin layer of fat surrounding the top of the meat, also called a "fat cap".

Trevor Janisse is an absolute tank. I first met Trevor when he was a culinary student at Niagara College and was planning a visit to Australia. His chef instructor sent him my way for advice and a list of places to eat. When Trevor came back, I was happy to have him on the truck as my right-hand man. He has the work ethic I'd love to see in any employee, but unfortunately we've lost him to the police service. We did manage to wrangle him into cooking for our wedding, and his beef brisket was a hit. Trevor has a true love of Southern cooking and barbecue. The Barbecue Sauce and Rub can be made up to three months in advance if desired.

Prepare Barbecue Sauce and set aside at room temperature until ready to use.

In a small bowl, combine all ingredients for Barbecue Rub. Mix well.

Apply Barbecue Rub to brisket, covering the entire surface of the meat. Set aside in the refrigerator.

In a small bowl, make a basting liquid by combining 2 Tbsp (30 mL) of Barbecue Sauce, water, and Worcestershire sauce. Mix well. Set aside.

Preheat smoker to 440°F (225°C).

Soak half of the hickory wood chips in cold water for approximately 20 minutes. Once soaked, mix the dry chips with the wet chips.

Feed the wood chips into the smoke box following the manufacturer's instructions, and top up with wood chips as required.

Place brisket in the smoker and let smoke for 15 to 18 hours. Every 3 hours, spray the brisket with basting liquid. Once cooked to an internal temperature of 350°F (180°C), remove brisket from smoker and place on a tray for approximately 30 minutes to rest.

Prepare the Slaw.

To serve, slice brisket thinly and make sandwiches by layering lean and fatty slices on egg buns. Cover with desired amount of Barbecue Sauce; any remaining can be saved for later. Top up with Slaw and serve immediately with a lot of cold beers!

→→ SERVES 4 OR MORE ←←

BARBECUE SAUCE

4 cups (1 L) canned crushed tomatoes,
  with juice
½ cup (125 mL) cider vinegar
2 Tbsp (30 mL) paprika
1 tsp (5 mL) ground cumin
1 tsp (5 mL) cayenne pepper
kosher salt, to taste
black pepper, freshly cracked, to taste

In a large stainless steel pot, combine all ingredients, and bring to a simmer over high heat. Reduce heat to medium, and cook for 1 hour or until sauce has reduced by half, stirring occasionally to stop the sauce from catching. Adjust the heat if required. Once reduced, remove from heat and allow to cool completely.

In a blender, purée sauce until smooth, and then pass sauce through a fine sieve.

Use immediately or transfer to an airtight container and store in the refrigerator for up to 3 months.

→ MAKES 2 CUPS (500 ML) ←

SLAW

½ green cabbage, finely chopped
¼ green bell pepper, finely sliced
1 small green onion, finely chopped
¾ cup (185 mL) white sugar
¾ cup (185 mL) white vinegar
½ tsp (2 mL) mustard seeds
½ tsp (2 mL) celery seeds
¼ cup (60 mL) canola oil

In a resealable container, combine cabbage, green pepper, and green onion. Mix to combine, and set aside at room temperature.

In a small pot, dissolve sugar in vinegar then add mustard and celery seeds; bring to a boil over high heat. Once boiled, pour liquid over cabbage mixture. Mix to coat the slaw, and then refrigerate for 8 to 12 hours.

→ MAKES 4 CUPS (1 L) ←

VIETNAMESE MARINATED BEEF SALAD

1 lb (500 g) beef tenderloin

½ cup (125 mL) bean sprouts

1 small white onion, finely diced

¼ English cucumber, seeded and
  finely julienned

¼ cup (60 mL) unsalted roasted peanuts

½ cup (125 mL) cilantro leaves

½ cup (125 mL) Thai basil leaves

3 bird's eye chilies, seeded
  and finely sliced

1¼-inches (3 cm) long piece ginger, peeled
  and finely julienned

juice of 6 limes

superfine sugar, to taste

fish sauce, to taste

¼ cup (60 mL) Fried Shallots (page 250)

This is a classic Vietnamese dish, where the beef is cooked in the acid of a marinade, much like how fish is cooked in a ceviche. The texture of the beef remains the same as though it was raw, but takes on the flavours of the marinade very quickly. It is a flavourful, fresh dish that is perfect for a hot summer night.

Finely slice the beef into roughly ⅟₃₂-inch (1 mm) thick slices. Place on a plate, and set aside in the refrigerator.

In a bowl, combine bean sprouts, onion, cucumber, peanuts, cilantro, basil, chilies, and ginger. Set aside at room temperature.

Place lime juice in a bowl, and add sugar and fish sauce, ½ tsp (2 mL) at a time, mixing to combine. Add additional sugar and fish sauce until you reach a balance of sour, sweet, and salty. Place the beef slices into the lime mixture, and allow to marinate in the refrigerator for approximately 5 minutes.

To serve, divide beef among the serving plates, arranging slices in a flat fan formation, overlapping slightly. Dress the salad with a small amount of the lime juice mixture, and toss to combine. Place a loose, neat pile of salad in the centre of the beef slices, and top with a scattering of Fried Shallots. Serve immediately.

→→ SERVES 4 ←←

RAS EL HANOUT BEEF SKEWERS

1 ¼ lb (625 g) beef strip loin, trimmed
  of fat and cut into ¾-inch (2 cm) cubes
½ cup (125 mL) sunflower oil
¼ cup (60 mL) Ras El Hanout (page 238)
juice of 2 lemons, divided
½ cup (125 mL) Labne (page 270)
8 button mushrooms, quartered
8 red shallots, quartered
kosher salt, to taste
black pepper, freshly cracked, to taste
1 head Boston lettuce, leaves picked

For this recipe I recommend using 8 large ornate kabob skewers. You can find them at most Middle Eastern grocery stores or online.

Ras el hanout is commonly used as a flavouring for tagines, or as a marinade for meat and fish. It imparts a very aromatic and robust, earthy flavour to this simple dish. Turn your next barbeque into a Moroccan feast! The spice blend's name *"Ras el hanout"* translates from Arabic to "head of the shop" or "top of the shelf" in English, and refers to the signature spice blends made by different spice vendors throughout Morocco. Every shop has its own blend, using the finest-quality spices. *Ras el hanout* can contain anywhere from 12 to 30 different spices. My blend has been tweaked over the years, but it originates from my previous chef, Cath Claringbold's, original blend.

In a resealable bag, place beef, oil, and Ras El Hanout. Set aside in the refrigerator for a minimum of 4 hours to marinate (the longer, the better).

In a small bowl, combine roughly three-quarters of the lemon juice and Labne. Mix well, and set aside in the refrigerator.

Preheat barbecue or indoor grill to highest setting.

Skewer the beef cubes, mushrooms, and shallots in an alternating pattern across the 8 skewers. Season with salt and pepper. Cook skewers on the barbecue turning occasionally, for 4 minutes total or until beef is medium-rare, while basting with remaining lemon juice.

Remove skewers from the barbecue and serve immediately with Boston lettuce leaf cups and lemon-*labne* mixture.

→→ SERVES 4 ←←

SEARED VENISON WITH CORN FRITTERS AND CHERRY GASTRIQUE

2 Tbsp (30 mL) cocoa nibs, ground

½ tsp (2 mL) coffee beans, freshly ground

1 tsp (5 mL) freshly cracked black pepper

1 tsp (5 mL) *fleur de sel*

1 tsp (5 mL) dried lemon myrtle

1 batch Corn Fritters (recipe follows)

1 Tbsp (15 mL) sunflower oil

1½ lb (750 g) whole venison
   tenderloin, trimmed

½ cup (125 mL) Cherry Gastrique
   (page 265)

½ cup (125 mL) sunflower shoots

Lemon myrtle, also known as lemon verbena, is a native Australian plant found in the northern tropical regions. It is used to make tea and dried seasonings and rubs. Lemon myrtle is available online or through specialty retailers.

Venison is a very lean game meat, so it is important not to overcook it. The cocoa and coffee in the rub helps to cut through the richness of the meat's flavour, while the sweetness from the corn fritters and cherry *gastrique* balances out the overall dish.

In a small bowl, combine cocoa nibs, coffee beans, pepper, *fleur de sel*, and lemon myrtle. Stir to combine, and set aside at room temperature.

Prepare Corn Fritters (see recipe next page). While fritters are cooking, heat oil in a heavy-bottomed skillet over high heat. Sear the tenderloins for approximately 1 minute on all sides, until cooked rare. Remove from skillet and place on a plate or tray, and let rest at room temperature for 1 minute.

Rub all sides of tenderloin with the cocoa nib mixture. Place tenderloin on a cutting board, and cut crosswise into ¾-inch (2 cm) thick slices.

To serve, place equal portions of tenderloin in a line along the middle of each serving plate. Place the corn fritters in a line beside the tenderloin, and dress with Cherry Gastrique. Garnish with sunflower shoots, and serve immediately.

→ SERVES 4 ←

Continued on next page

Continued from previous page

CORN FRITTERS

4 cups (1 L) canola oil

4 ears corn, shucked

1 clove garlic

2 red shallots

1 kaffir lime leaf, spine removed

1 bird's eye chili, seeded

2-inches (5 cm) long piece ginger, peeled
   and roughly chopped

2 large eggs

2 cups (500 mL) self-rising flour,
   more if needed

In a large pot, heat oil to 350°F (180°C).

Using a sharp knife, cut kernels from corn cobs. Place kernels, garlic, shallots, lime leaf, chili, and ginger into a blender. Purée until smooth. Transfer mixture to a bowl, and set aside at room temperature.

Crack eggs into a separate small bowl and whisk well.

Add whisked eggs to corn mixture. Mix thoroughly. Add flour gradually to corn mixture, and combine. Be careful not to over-work, as mixture will become doughy after cooking.

 NOTE *Batter should be thick, similar to pancake batter.*

Carefully drop tablespoon-sized portions of corn batter into hot oil. Deep-fry for 2 to 3 minutes or until golden brown and cooked in the centre. Remove fritters from the pot, and place on paper towel to absorb excess oil.

VENISON SAUSAGES WITH GARLICKY KALE

RECIPE BY GUEST CHEF: MIKE MCCOLL, PHOTOS WITH SAUCE, BURLINGTON, ONTARIO

SAUSAGES

½ cup (125 mL) rendered duck fat

10 small cloves garlic

1 large white onion, cut into ½-inch
   (1 cm) cubes

2 tsp (10 mL) + 2 Tbsp (30 mL) kosher salt

1 tsp (5 mL) freshly ground black pepper

1 tsp (5 mL) cumin seeds

1 tsp (5 mL) celery seeds

1 Tbsp (15 mL) paprika

1 cup (250 mL) flat leaf parsley leaves

¼ cup (60 mL) sage leaves

3 lb (1.5 kg) venison shoulder, cut into
   1½-inch (4 cm) cubes

3 lb (1.5 kg) pork shoulder, cut into
   1½-inch (4 cm) cubes

1 lb (500 g) pork back fat, cut into
   1½-inch (4 cm) cubes

25 ft (7.5 m) sausage casings (approx.)

ENTRÉE

2 Tbsp (30 mL) unsalted butter, divided

5 cloves garlic, minced

1 small onion, minced

½ yellow or orange bell pepper, minced

1 cup (250 mL) chicken (or venison) stock
   (approx.), divided

2 bunches kale, roughly torn into
   approximately 3-inch (8 cm) squares

kosher salt, to taste

black pepper, freshly cracked, to taste

Mike McColl is both a skilled and avid griller and a fan of all things meat. Over the last couple of years, Mike has been making sausages with his buddy Bill, who is a hunter. Mike and Bill get together after a venison hunt to experiment with sausages and cured meats.

These sausages freeze well, so while you have all the equipment out and running, don't be afraid to make some extras for the freezer. This recipe works best if you have a food grinder attachment and a sausage stuffer attachment for your stand mixer. I like to grind my own meat, but you can ask your butcher to grind it fresh for you.

TO MAKE THE SAUSAGES, in a large skillet, heat duck fat over medium heat for approximately 2 minutes. Add garlic, onion, 2 tsp (10 mL) of salt, pepper, cumin seeds, and celery seeds. Sauté, stirring frequently, for 25 to 30 minutes or until the mixture has a nice golden-brown, caramelized colour. Stir in paprika, parsley, and sage. Cook for an additional 2 minutes or until herbs have wilted. Remove from heat, and set aside at room temperature to cool completely.

Set up your meat grinder according to the manufacturer's instructions. Grind the venison, pork, pork back fat, and the onion mixture into a large bowl, and season with 2 Tbsp (30 mL) of salt. Wearing gloves, use your hands to combine the sausage mixture and distribute the ingredients thoroughly.

 I like to finish the grinding by feeding a slice of bread through the grinder, which pushes out any of the remaining good stuff left inside the grinder.

Refrigerate the mixture until you are ready to stuff the sausages, or for a maximum of 24 hours.

Take a 1–2 oz (30–60 g) portion of the sausage mixture and form it into a loose burger patty. In a small frying pan over medium-high heat, fry the patty for 1 to 2 minutes or until fully cooked through. Remove from pan and taste for seasoning. Season to taste and mix thoroughly.

Set up your sausage stuffer according to the manufacturer's instructions. Slide a section of sausage casing onto the stuffer nozzle and begin the stuffing process, twisting off each link in a uniform length, about 8–10 inches (20–25 cm) per sausage. Repeat as necessary with the rest of the casings until the sausage mixture is used up.

Continued on next page

Continued from previous page

You can get rendered duck fat from your butcher or specialty meat retailer.

If you can't find sausage casings at your butcher shop, you can make patties from the same recipe.

 Alternate the twists every link or you will unravel your previous twists. This may take a minute to sink in, but you will get the hang of it.

Refrigerate sausages until you are ready to cook or freeze for up to 3 months. To freeze, cut into single or double links and place in a single layer in a resealable bag.

TO MAKE THE ENTRÉE, in a heavy non-stick skillet or cast iron pan with a fitted lid, melt 1 Tbsp (15 mL) of butter over medium heat. Fry 6 sausages for 8 to 10 minutes per side or until golden brown and reach an internal temperature of 160°F (70°C). Remove from pan and set aside at room temperature while you cook the kale.

Increase the heat to high and add remaining 1 Tbsp (15 mL) of butter to the pan. Add the garlic, onion, and bell pepper, and stir constantly for 2 minutes or until vegetables have softened but not browned. Add ½ cup (125 mL) of the stock and the kale and cover with the lid. Sweat the kale for 3 to 4 minutes, stirring occasionally to ensure an even cook and adding more stock as needed to keep it steaming, not frying. Season with salt and pepper. Place the sausages back into the pan (with any juice that has leeched onto the resting plate), cover, and cook for an additional 2 minutes. Remove from heat, and serve immediately with your favourite starch.

→ MAKES 20–24 SAUSAGES ←

LAMB SOUVLAKI

RECIPE BY GUEST CHEF: CATH CLARINGBOLD, BURCH & PURCHESE SWEET STUDIO, MELBOURNE, AUSTRALIA

2 tsp (10 mL) Dijon mustard

1 cup (250 mL) olive oil

2 tsp (10 mL) *rigani*

6 large sprigs thyme, roughly chopped

6 large sprigs rosemary, roughly chopped

5 cloves garlic, crushed

juice of 2 lemons

1 3 lb (1.5 kg) deboned lamb
  shoulder (approx.)

kosher salt, to taste

black pepper, freshly cracked, to taste

12 Pita Breads (page 254)

Tzatziki, to taste (page 273)

1 white onion, finely sliced

2 beefsteak tomatoes, diced

2 cups (500 mL) arugula

> You can find *rigani* at most Middle Eastern grocers.
>
> Prepare the lamb in the marinade at least 12 hours in advance of cooking.
>
> Remove some of the excess fat from the lamb shoulder, but not all of it.

Cath Claringbold now works alongside her husband, Darren Purchese, at Burch & Purchese. Cath took me on for the second half of my apprenticeship at MECCA Restaurant in Melbourne. If I had the chance to repeat my career, I wouldn't change a thing because of the opportunity to work under Cath. The way Cath worked, and her kitchen demeanour, is inspiring and has shaped me as a chef. I'll never forget the night when, in the middle of one of the busiest services at MECCA, I looked over the middle of the range to read the memos on the board. Cath caught my gaze and asked, in the calmest of voices, "How ya goin', Adz? You good?" Her section was being absolutely pounded, she never lost a beat, and I knew she had my back. I have always tried to be that calm in the kitchen in the middle of a busy service, and I keep that thought in my head during service if things get hairy.

In a large bowl, combine mustard, oil, *rigani*, thyme, rosemary, garlic, and lemon juice. Mix well. Add the lamb and coat it all over with the marinade. Cover and place in the refrigerator for a minimum of 12 hours to marinate.

Preheat oven to 275–300°F (140–150°C).

Lay the marinated meat on a roasting tray and season well with salt and pepper, and place in the oven. Baste the meat from time to time with the cooking juices. Cook until the meat reaches an internal temperature of 125–135°F (50–60°C) and is completely tender. Depending on the thickness of the lamb, this can take 2 to 4 hours. When the meat is cooked, remove from the oven and let rest for 20 minutes before carving or pulling apart.

Serve family-style with warm Pita Breads, Tzatziki, onions, tomatoes, and arugula.

→ SERVES 4 OR MORE, DEPENDING ON HOW MUCH LAMB YOUR GUESTS EAT WITH THEIR PITAS ←

LAMB LADY'S FINGERS

¼ cup (60 mL) full-fat Greek yogurt

1 cup (250 mL) mint leaves

¼ cup (60 mL) flat leaf parsley leaves

1 cup (250 mL) Labne (page 270)

juice of 1 lemon

kosher salt, to taste

black pepper, freshly cracked, to taste

1 Tbsp (15 mL) olive oil

1 small yellow onion, finely diced

2 cloves garlic, finely chopped

1 Tbsp (15 mL) ground allspice

½ Tbsp (7 mL) cayenne powder

½ Tbsp (7 mL) ground cinnamon

½ Tbsp (7 mL) ground ginger

2.2 lb (1 kg) ground lamb shoulder

½ cup (125 mL) water (approx.)

¼ cup (60 mL) pine nuts, toasted,
 finely chopped

½ cup (125 mL) cilantro leaves,
 finely chopped

12 sheets phyllo pastry

¼ cup (60 mL) unsalted butter, melted

2 eggs

4 cups (1 L) canola oil

2 Tbsp (30 mL) Za'atar (page 238)

Lady's fingers are served family-style along with the rest of the meal in Lebanon. This recipe is inspired by my time working at MECCA Restaurant in Melbourne. I remember having to make hundreds of these little things daily. So many lady's fingers . . . so many.

In a blender, purée yogurt, mint, and parsley until very smooth. Set aside at room temperature.

Place Labne in a small bowl, and add blender contents. Whisk to combine, and add lemon juice. Season with salt and pepper, and whisk further. Set aside in the refrigerator.

In a large, flat-bottomed pot, heat olive oil over high heat. Add onion, and fry for 3 minutes or until onions catch on the bottom of the pot and become translucent, stirring occasionally. Add garlic and spices, and stir to combine. Cook for an additional 1 minute.

Add lamb, and mix to combine well. Allow lamb to cook long enough to catch on the bottom of the pot in between stirring. Deglaze the pot with approximately 2 Tbsp (30 mL) of water, and scratch the browned bits from the bottom of the pot with a wooden spoon. Allow pot to come back to high heat, and cook for approximately 5 minutes to allow all of the liquid to cook out. Repeat the process of allowing the lamb to catch on the bottom, deglazing with water, and cooking out liquid 5 to 6 times.

Once the liquid is cooked after the final deglazing, remove from heat. Add the pine nuts and cilantro, and mix well. Season to taste with salt and pepper. Transfer the lamb mixture to a tray. Set aside and allow to cool to room temperature.

Carefully lay one sheet of phyllo pastry on a clean, cool work surface. Using a pastry brush, gently brush the entire surface of the phyllo with melted butter. Place a second sheet of phyllo on top, being careful not to trap too many air bubbles in between the sheets of phyllo. Set the glued phyllo to the side, and cover with a tea towel. Repeat this process with remaining sheets of pastry, for a total of 6 pairs of glued sheets.

Arrange the glued pairs of sheets in a neat stack. Using a sharp knife, cut the stack of sheets into four equal sections, crosswise, creating rectangles.

In a small bowl, whisk the eggs with a fork, and set aside at room temperature.

Carefully lay out 4 rectangles of glued phyllo on a clean work surface. Spoon a manageable amount, approximately 1 Tbsp (15 mL), of lamb mixture onto the bottom third of each phyllo rectangle, leaving at least ½ inch (1 cm) of space along the left and right edges, and the edge closest to you.

Using your finger or a very small pastry brush, lightly paint a small line of egg wash along the left and right edges of each of the phyllo rectangles. Fold the left and right edges over the lamb mixture, pressing the edges down to form a neat seam along the length of the phyllo rectangles.

Working with one rectangle of phyllo at a time, fold the edge of the phyllo that is closest to you over the lamb mixture, and gently but firmly roll the lady's finger, leaving ½ inch (1 cm) of phyllo exposed at the top. Lightly wash the top edge of the phyllo with egg wash and finish rolling the lady's finger. Press gently but firmly to seal the roll. Cover rolled fingers with a tea towel while you repeat the process with the remaining rectangles until all of the lamb mixture has been used.

 Lady's fingers can be frozen at this point to be cooked later or can be cooked immediately.

In a heavy-bottomed pot, heat canola oil to 350°F (180°C).

Fry pastries for 2 to 3 minutes or until golden brown. Remove from the pot and place on paper towel to absorb excess oil.

To serve, spoon equal portions of mint *labne* on each serving plate, and push the *labne* to create a line across the plate. Place 6 ladyfingers crosswise along the *labne* on each plate. Sprinkle liberally with Za'atar, and serve immediately.

→ SERVES 4 ←

LAMB TARTARE WITH CHERMOULA

1 lb (500 g) lamb loin, trimmed
 of visible sinew
2 small red shallots, finely diced
3 Tbsp (45 mL) cornichons, finely diced
2 Tbsp (30 mL) parmesan cheese,
 finely grated
1 egg yolk
3 Tbsp (45 mL) Wet Chermoula (approx.)
 (page 234)
kosher salt, to taste
black pepper, freshly cracked, to taste
1 Tbsp (15 mL) chives, finely sliced
1 Tbsp (15 mL) Fried Shallots (page 250)
1 Tbsp (15 mL) Fried Garlic (page 251)
16 Pickled Radishes (page 242), quartered
1 head Boston lettuce, leaves picked

Raw lamb has a beautifully sweet flavour, and the addition of wet chermoula balances this sweetness with heat, earthiness, and sourness. Lettuce cups add a refreshing crispness to each bite. If raw lamb is something you aren't keen on, try replacing the lamb with beef.

Place a very clean cutting board in the refrigerator, and allow to cool for approximately 10 minutes.

While the cutting board is chilling, place 2 handfuls of ice in a medium bowl. Nestle a smaller bowl into the ice, and place bowls in the refrigerator.

Return the chilled cutting board to your work surface. Wearing gloves and using a very sharp knife, finely slice the lamb crosswise into disks. Finely dice sliced lamb, and transfer crosswise to chilled bowl.

Add the shallots, cornichons, parmesan, and egg yolk to the lamb. Add Wet Chermoula and combine thoroughly. Taste, and add more Wet Chermoula if desired. Season with salt and pepper.

To serve, spoon equal portions of tartare in the centre of each serving plate. Using the back of a large spoon, press down on the centre of the tartare to create a flat, wide surface. Sprinkle the entire surface of the tartare with the chives, Fried Shallots, and Fried Garlic. Serve immediately with Pickled Radishes and lettuce cups on the side.

→ SERVES 4 ←

LAMB SKEWERS WITH TOUM

1 small yellow onion
2.2 lb (1 kg) ground lamb shoulder
5 Tbsp (75 mL) Kofta Spice (page 237)
½ cup (125 mL) mint leaves,
 finely chopped
kosher salt, to taste
black pepper, freshly cracked, to taste
¼ cup (60 mL) grape seed oil
½ cup (125 mL) Chili Mint Relish
 (page 267)
¼ cup (60 mL) Toum (page 274)
1 head Boston lettuce, leaves picked

> The word "*kofta*" is used to refer to a variety of shaped, spiced meats, from meatballs in Morocco to kabobs in Turkey.

Mint and lamb is a classic combination. In this recipe, this combination gets a vibrant lift from the intense garlic and spiciness of the *toum*. Originating in Egypt, *toum* is a dip or sauce traditionally served with meats. For something more substantial and portable, consider serving this dish in pitas with additional trimmings of your choice. I like to use ornate metal skewers that can be found at Middle Eastern grocery stores, but any kind will work, as long as you have 12 of them.

Using a box grater over a bowl, grate the onion on the smallest grater. Set aside at room temperature.

In a separate bowl, combine lamb, Kofta Spice, onion, and mint. Season with salt and pepper. Set aside in the refrigerator.

Wearing gloves, form 3-inch (8 cm) long sausage-like lengths of lamb mixture around the pointy end of the kabob skewers. Store on a tray in the refrigerator.

Preheat barbecue or indoor grill to the highest possible setting.

Brush the *kofta* with oil, and carefully place on the grill. Once placed, allow *kofta* to char slightly before rotating a quarter turn. Repeat this process until all sides of the *kofta* are lightly charred, and *kofta* are cooked to roughly a medium doneness. Cooking time will depend on the thickness of your *kofta*.

Once cooked, remove *kofta* from grill and place on a clean tray. Allow to rest at room temperature for approximately 3 minutes. Serve immediately with Chili Mint Relish, Toum, and lettuce cups on the side.

→ SERVES 4 ←

KOFTA AND EGG TAGINE

5 red shallots, finely diced

¼ cup (60 mL) Kofta Spice (page 237)

1¼ lb (625 g) ground lamb shoulder

1 cup (250 mL) cilantro leaves, finely
  chopped, divided

kosher salt, to taste

1 Tbsp (15 mL) sunflower oil

12 Roma tomatoes

1 Tbsp (15 mL) canola oil

1 small yellow onion, finely diced

3 cloves garlic, finely chopped

1 tsp (5 mL) ground ginger

½ tsp (2 mL) ground cinnamon

1 cup (250 mL) crushed canned tomatoes

3 Tbsp (45 mL) Harissa (page 231)

honey, to taste

4 eggs

¼ cup (60 mL) pine nuts, toasted

4 Pita Breads (page 254)

> To toast pine nuts, preheat oven to 350°F (180°C). Place pine nuts in a tray or a small pan and toast in oven, tossing occasionally until golden brown, 4 to 6 minutes.

Kofta is a spiced ground lamb mix, which differs in its ingredients between countries in North Africa and into the Middle Eastern/Baltic regions. The eggs in this dish are essentially poached in the aromatic sauce as they cook, and are broken up and mixed through the tagine after serving.

Ideally, this dish should be plated in traditional clay tagines (the food is named after the dish it is served in), but we have also served it on the street with slight modifications to the plating. Use cooking tagines for this, not ornamental. You can find traditional clay cooking tagines at Middle Eastern grocers or online from specialty retailers. You will need either four small heat-proof tagines or one very large heat-proof tagine.

In a bowl, combine shallots, Kofta Spice, ground lamb, and two-thirds of the cilantro. Season with salt, and mix well. Heat sunflower oil in a small skillet over high heat. Form a small meatball with the lamb mixture, and cook on all sides in the skillet. Taste the cooked lamb for seasoning, and adjust remaining lamb mixture if needed.

Divide the lamb mixture into 20 equally sized portions, and form tight, uniform meatballs. Place on a tray, and store in the refrigerator.

Heat water in a pot over high heat. Bring to a boil. Remove the core from the Roma tomatoes, and score the skin on the opposite end with a paring knife. Place the tomatoes in the boiling water, and count to 10. Turn off heat, carefully remove tomatoes from water, and place them in a sieve. Run the tomatoes under cold water until chilled, approximately 2 minutes. Peel the skin from the chilled tomatoes, and cut into quarters lengthwise. Remove the seeds, and finely dice the tomatoes. Set aside.

To make the sauce, heat canola oil in a pot over medium-high heat. Sweat the onion for approximately 5 minutes. Add the garlic, and sweat for an additional 2 minutes. Add the ginger and cinnamon, and cook for an additional 2 minutes, continuing to stir. Add the crushed tomatoes and diced Roma tomatoes. Bring sauce to a boil. Once boiling, reduce heat to medium-high and simmer, stirring occasionally, for 30 to 45 minutes or until thickened. Add Harissa and season to taste with honey and salt.

Preheat oven to 525°F (275°C) or highest setting.

Portion sauce equally into the bases of the tagines. Divide lamb meatballs equally among the tagine, submerging halfway in sauce. Crack 1 egg into the centre of each tagine. Place, uncovered, in the oven, and cook for 12 minutes or until the eggs and meatballs are cooked.

Garnish with a sprinkling of remaining cilantro and pine nuts. Cover tagines with lids, and serve with Pita Breads.

→ SERVES 4 ←

CRISPY PIG TONGUES WITH PICKLED FENNEL

8 cups (2 L) water

2 cups (500 mL) white vinegar

1 large yellow onion, roughly chopped

¼ cup (60 mL) kosher salt

¼ cup (60 mL) whole black peppercorns

4 pig tongues

2 large eggs, whisked

½ cup (125 mL) whole milk

½ cup (125 mL) Dukkah (page 237)

4 cups (1 L) panko bread crumbs

1 cup (250 mL) all-purpose flour

4 cups (1 L) canola oil

kosher salt, to taste

black pepper, freshly cracked, to taste

8 wedges of Pickled Fennel (page 245)

½ cup (125 mL) Chili Mint Relish (page 267)

4 lemon wedges

El Gastrónomo Vagabundo was featured on season three of the popular TV series *Eat St.*, and one of the dishes we served during the episode was Dukkah-Crumbed Lamb Tongue with Shaved Fennel and Chili Mint Relish. When I first put this dish on the menu, it took a little convincing and a lot of free samples for the fearful to see the light. Gradually, customers caught on to how tender and delicious pickled tongue can be, reminiscent of the more familiar corned beef. It became a very popular dish, but due to the difficulty of sourcing lamb tongue in mass quantities, it hasn't returned to the menu since. Instead, I started using pig tongue, which is more widely available. The dish itself has evolved since it first went on the menu, with pickling the fennel, and the way it is plated. It is still a hugely popular dish, though it only appears on the menu on rare occasions. You will have to prepare the pig tongues one day in advance to allow for thorough chilling after the pickling process.

In a large stainless steel pot, bring water, vinegar, onion, salt, and peppercorns to a boil over high heat.

Rinse pig tongues under cold water to wash off any package juices. Place tongues in pickling liquid, and bring back to a boil. Reduce heat to medium and simmer for 1½ hours or until pig tongues are fork-tender.

 NOTE *You should be able to gently press a skewer through the tongues without any resistance.*

Once cooked, remove from heat and use a slotted spoon to transfer tongues to a tray to cool slightly. While still warm but not too hot to handle, peel the skin from the tongues. Place tongues back in the cooked pickling liquid, and allow to cool to room temperature. Once cooled, place in the refrigerator, covered with a lid, overnight.

Remove tongues from pickling liquid and place on a clean cutting board. Working with one tongue at a time, begin at the tip of the tongue and use a sharp knife to slice the tongues into ¼-inch (6 mm) thick disks. Set sliced tongue meat aside at room temperature.

In a small bowl, combine eggs and milk. In a separate small bowl, combine Dukkah and panko. Set up a crumbing station, with flour, egg-milk mixture, and *dukkah*-panko each in separate bowls, in that order.

Continued on next page

Continued from previous page

In a large, heavy-bottomed pot, heat oil to 350°F (180°C).

Dredge tongue slices in flour, then soak in egg-milk mixture before transferring to *dukkah*-panko bowl. Evenly coat the tongue slices in *dukkah*-panko mix, and set aside on a plate in the refrigerator.

Working in batches, carefully place *dukkah*-crumbed tongue slices in the hot oil, and cook for 3 minutes or until golden brown. Remove cooked tongues from pot, and place on paper towel to absorb excess oil. Repeat this process until all slices of tongue are fried. Season with salt and pepper.

To serve, cut each fennel quarter in half lengthwise, and place two pieces in the centre of each serving plate. Neatly stack equal portions of pig tongue on and around the fennel. Serve with Chili Mint Relish and a lemon wedge on the side.

→→ SERVES 4 ←←

BABI IN A BOWL

RECIPE BY GUEST CHEF: CINDY ARMAN, BABI & CO., TORONTO, ONTARIO

2.2 lb (1 kg) pork belly, cut into ¾-inch (2 cm) cubes

¼ cup (60 mL) garlic, minced

¼ cup (60 mL) *kecap manis*

½ tsp (2 mL) white sugar

1 tsp (5 mL) light soy sauce

½ tsp (2 mL) kosher salt

½ tsp (2 mL) white pepper

3 Tbsp (45 mL) canola oil

4 cloves garlic, smashed with skin on

4 hard-boiled eggs, peeled

4 cups (1 L) steamed jasmine rice

1 Tbsp (15 mL) Fried Shallots (page 250)

1 bird's eye chili, finely sliced

½ cup (125 mL) cilantro leaves

1 medium Kirby (pickling) cucumber, finely sliced

Kecap manis, also known as Indonesian sweet soy sauce, is available at most Asian grocers.

Cindy Arman is the founder of Babi & Co., an Indonesian street-food pop-up restaurant based in Toronto. Cindy is extremely talented, hard working, and focussed. She has offered many times to help out on the truck. Cindy is always smiling and happy, which shows through in her food.

In a large stainless steel bowl, combine the pork belly, garlic, *kecap manis*, sugar, soy sauce, salt, and pepper. Mix well, and place in the refrigerator for 1 hour to marinate.

In a wok, heat the oil over high heat. Add smashed garlic along with the skin, stirring constantly, and cook for 30 seconds or until golden brown. Add the marinated pork, stir to combine, and fry for 8 to 10 minutes. Reduce heat to medium-low and add the hard-boiled eggs. Simmer for 5 to 8 minutes or until sauce has thickened.

To serve, place cooked pork mixture over steamed rice, and place a whole boiled egg in the bowl. Garnish with Fried Shallots, sliced chili, cilantro, and cucumber.

→ SERVES 4 ←

MASTER STOCK BRAISED PORK BELLY WITH GREEN PAPAYA SALAD

½ boneless, skin-on pork belly
12 cups (3 L) Master Stock (page 263)
4 cups (1 L) canola oil
1 batch Green Papaya Salad (page 22)
1 cup (250 mL) Chili Caramel (page 265)

You will need butcher's twine for this recipe.

One of my all-time favourite dishes, this recipe has evolved over the years to its current incarnation. It is inspired by a dish I learned from Chef Nick Anthony when he was chef-owner of The Bridge Hotel in Bendigo, Australia. I learned specific techniques used in this recipe from Nick, like rolling and braising the pork belly, and the basics of the Chili Caramel lacquer.

Pork belly is the cut of the pig that is used to make bacon. When buying pork belly for this recipe, ask your butcher to cut a whole belly in half widthwise and, if possible, to burn off any remaining hair from the skin.

Lay the pork belly, flesh side down, on a cutting board, with the butcher's cut to the right side. Using a very sharp knife, score the skin horizontally from left to right, with score marks spaced approximately ½ inch (1.5 cm) apart. Flip the pork belly over, keeping the butcher's cut side on the right.

Cut a length of butcher's twine at least 6.5 feet (2 m) long. Very tightly roll the pork belly upwards from the bottom edge, so that the score marks run in the same direction as the length of the roll.

With the belly roll placed horizontally in front of you, begin at the leftmost edge of the roll. Pass one end of the twine underneath the roll, 1 inch (2.5 cm) from the edge of the roll. Cross the ends of the twine on top of the roll, and tie a knot. Trim the shorter length of excess twine close to the knot. Hold the remaining, longer string above the meat with your left hand, and loop it around your right hand.

Using your right hand, slide the loop under the belly roll, pulling the twine tight with your left hand until the loop is snugly in place 1 inch (2.5 cm) from the first loop. Make a knot to secure the new loop. Repeat every 1 inch (2.5 cm), making evenly spaced and knotted loops, until you reach the right end of the belly roll. Tie the end of the twine tightly, and cut the excess twine close to the last knot.

In a large pot, bring Master Stock to a boil over high heat. Place trussed pork belly in stock. Bring stock back to a boil, then adjust heat to medium. Simmer for 1½ hours or until pork belly is cooked through.

 You should be able to gently press a skewer through the belly without any resistance.

Continued on next page

Continued from page 102

Remove stock pot from heat. Using a spider or slotted spoon, transfer the rolled pork belly to a tray and allow to cool to room temperature. Once cooled, place in the refrigerator to chill completely.

Once chilled, cut the butcher's twine from the pork belly, ensuring all twine is removed. Using a very sharp knife, cut the pork into ½-inch (1 cm) disks. Set aside in the refrigerator.

Prepare the Green Papaya Salad, without dressing it with Nuoc Mam or garnishing at this time. Set aside at room temperature.

In a heavy-bottomed pot, heat oil to 350°F (180°C).

In a large bowl, place Chili Caramel, and set aside for coating the pork once it is fried.

Working in batches, fry the pork belly disks for 4 minutes or until slightly crispy. Remove pork from pot, allowing excess fat to drain, and set on paper towel to absorb excess fat. Place fried pork belly in the Chili Caramel bowl and toss to coat. Repeat this process until all of the pork belly is fried and coated with Chili Caramel.

To serve, place a disk of pork belly in the centre of each serving plate. Dress the Green Papaya Salad with Nuoc Mam, and toss to combine. Place equal portions of salad in a neat nest on top of each serving of pork belly. As per the Green Papaya Salad recipe, add garnishes now. Serve immediately.

→→ SERVES 4 WITH LEFTOVER PORK BELLY ←←

MASTER STOCK BRAISED PORK HOCK BAO

8 cups (2 L) Master Stock (page 263)

2 smoked pork hocks

16 Steamed Buns (page 255)

4 cups (1 L) canola oil

½ cup (125 mL) Chili Caramel (page 265)

¼ cup (60 mL) Five Spice (page 233)

6 green onions, halved lengthwise and
cut into 1-inch (2.5 cm) segments

1 English cucumber, finely sliced
into disks

1 cup (250 mL) Chili Jam (page 266)

1 cup (250 mL) cilantro leaves

2 limes, cut into wedges

Smoked pork hocks are available at delicatessens or specialty butchers.

Steamed buns, or *bao*, are a traditional street food from China and are as versatile as sandwiches in Western culture. When we first opened the food truck, we served our take on this classic dish with five-spiced pork belly and chili jam. This recipe is an evolution of our first take on *bao* and uses sticky, tender pork hock in place of the pork belly.

In a large pot, combine Master Stock and smoked pork hocks. Bring to a simmer over high heat, and cook for 45 minutes or until the pork hock is tender and close to falling off the bone.

Using a spider or slotted spoon, remove cooked hocks from stock. Place on a tray to cool at room temperature, and then transfer to the refrigerator to cool completely. Follow the directions in the Master Stock recipe for storing the stock for future use.

Once cooled, remove and discard excess fat and skin from hocks. Break the meat off the bones in large chunks for frying. Set aside in the refrigerator.

Prepare Steamed Buns recipe and steamer baskets.

In a large stainless steel pot, heat oil to 350°F (180°C).

Deep-fry chunks of pork in the hot oil for 2½ minutes. Remove from pot and place in a stainless steel bowl. Coat with Chili Caramel, and sprinkle evenly with Five Spice, tossing to coat. Set aside at room temperature.

Once buns are cooked, serve immediately, family-style. Place pork hock, green onions, cucumber, Chili Jam, cilantro, and lime wedges in separate serving dishes, and serve with steamed buns. Build your *bao* to taste with the pork hock, Chili Jam, and fresh garnishes.

» SERVES 4 «

CHICKEN POT STICKERS

4 dried shiitake mushrooms

3 cups (750 mL) unbleached
  all-purpose flour

1⅛ cups (280 mL) just-boiled
  water (approx.)

1 lb (500 g) ground chicken breast

6 water chestnuts, shelled and
  finely diced

2-inches (5 cm) long piece ginger, peeled
  and finely diced

5 red shallots, finely diced

3 cloves garlic, finely diced

kosher salt, to taste

black pepper, freshly cracked, to taste

2 Tbsp (30 mL) sunflower oil

¼ cup (60 mL) hot water

Pot stickers are a steamed dumpling that is fried on one side before steaming, which gives the pot stickers simultaneously a crisp and soft steamed texture, giving dumpling fans the best of both worlds. Variations of pot stickers are found throughout China, Korea, and Japan.

Soak mushrooms in warm water for 20 minutes. Squeeze them to remove excess water and finely slice. Set aside.

To make the dough, place flour in a mixing bowl or a stand mixer with the dough hook attachment. On low speed, gradually add the just-boiled water to the flour. Let the dough hook bring the dough together, stopping to scrape the sides of the mixing bowl as needed. Once all of the water is added, make sure all of the flour has been incorporated, and continue to knead with the dough hook for an additional 2 minutes. Add more water by the teaspoonful if mixture is too dry and crumbly.

Place dough on a lightly floured surface. Knead by hand for 30 seconds to 1 minute, ensuring the dough is smooth. Place in a resealable bag, expelled of air. Allow to sit at room temperature for a minimum of 2 hours.

When dough is ready, remove it from the bag and cover with a moist tea towel. Cut off tablespoon-sized pieces of dough and roll them out on a lightly floured surface, one at a time. Stack rolled dough portions with pieces of plastic wrap in between, dusted lightly with flour. Repeat this process until all of the dough has been rolled.

In a bowl, combine chicken, water chestnuts, sliced mushrooms, ginger, shallots, and garlic. Season with salt and pepper. Mix well, and set aside at room temperature.

Continued on next page

Continued from page 110

Working with one piece of rolled dough at a time, place a spoonful of chicken mixture in the centre of the dough. Use your finger to brush the edges of the dough with water. Fold the dough over so the edges meet, forming a moon-shaped dumpling. Pinch edges to seal the dumpling. Beginning at one end of the dumpling, use your fingers to slightly overlap the edge of the dumpling with itself, pinching as you go to create a series of Z-shaped folds along the outside edge. Repeat this process with the remaining dough, covering the dumplings with a tea towel or plastic wrap as you go.

To cook pot stickers, heat oil in a large skillet over medium-high heat. Place dumplings into the skillet, flat side down, and fry for 2 to 3 minutes or until golden brown. Do not flip. Pour in hot water, cover with a tight-fitting lid, and cook for an additional 2 to 3 minutes or until cooked through.

Serve immediately with your favourite dipping sauces.

→→ SERVES 4 ←←

Continued from previous page

CHICKEN SKIN GRAVY

2.2 lb (1 kg) chicken skins
1 small yellow onion, diced
1 stalk celery, diced
1 carrot, diced
2 Tbsp (30 mL) unsalted butter
1 sprig thyme
½ cup (125 mL) flat leaf parsley leaves
6 whole black peppercorns
2 whole allspice
1 sprig sage
1 clove garlic
2 bay leaves
2 cups (500 mL) white wine
4 cups (1 L) Brown Chicken Stock
  (page 260)
2 cups (500 mL) heavy cream

This recipe yields approximately 4 cups (1 L) of gravy. Extra gravy can be refrigerated in an airtight container for up to 1 week, or frozen for up to 6 months.

Preheat oven to 400°F (200°C).

Place chicken skins on a baking sheet lined with a silicone mat, and roast for 45 minutes or until golden brown, checking every so often and rotating tray. Once cooked, remove from oven, and set aside at room temperature, reserving the rendered fat.

In a large pot, sauté onions, celery, and carrots in butter over medium-high heat for approximately 10 minutes. Stir occasionally so as not to burn. Add thyme, parsley, peppercorns, allspice, sage, garlic, bay leaves, roasted chicken skins, and reserved chicken fat. Stir to combine. Add wine, and simmer for 20 minutes or until it is almost entirely evaporated. Add stock, and simmer for 1 to 1½ hours or until sauce thickens to the consistency of jam.

Once the sauce has thickened, add heavy cream and reduce gently for approximately 10 minutes over medium-low heat. Remove from the heat and, using the back of a ladle, pass the sauce through a fine sieve, discarding the solids.

Use immediately or transfer to an airtight container and store in the refrigerator for up to 1 week or freeze for up to 6 months.

→ MAKES 4 CUPS (1 L) ←

GOAT CHEESE CREAM

3½ oz (100 g) goat cheese
½ cup (125 mL) heavy cream
½ tsp (2 mL) Five Spice (page 233)
kosher salt, to taste

In a small bowl, combine goat cheese, cream, and Five Spice. Season with salt.

Use immediately or transfer to an airtight container and store in the refrigerator for up to 1 week.

→ MAKES JUST UNDER 1 CUP (225 ML) ←

FRIED CHICKEN AND CANDIED BACON WAFFLES

8 boneless, skinless chicken thighs

4 cups (1 L) Master Stock (page 263)

2 large eggs

1¾ cups (435 mL) whole milk

½ cup (125 mL) sunflower oil

5 cups (1.25 L) all-purpose flour, divided

4 tsp (20 mL) baking powder

¼ tsp (1 mL) + 1 Tbsp (15 mL) kosher salt

½ cup (125 mL) roughly chopped Candied
  Bacon (page 249)

4 cups (1 L) canola oil

1 tsp (5 mL) ground star anise

1 tsp (5 mL) ground cinnamon

1 tsp (5 mL) ground ginger

1 tsp (5 mL) freshly cracked black pepper

½ cup (125 mL) Toasted Coconut Cream
  (page 273)

½ cup (125 mL) Chili Caramel (page 265)

1 cup (250 mL) cilantro leaves

Chicken should be brined in
Master Stock 2 days ahead
of serving.

You will need a waffle iron.

Fried chicken and waffles is a popular soul food dish in the southern United States. The popularity of this dish has expanded worldwide, with chefs adding their own personal touches. I serve chicken and waffles with Toasted Coconut Cream and Chili Caramel for a Thai-style take on the traditional butter and maple syrup.

Place chicken in a large resealable container, and cover completely with Master Stock. Cover container with lid and place in the refrigerator for approximately 2 days.

On the day of cooking, prepare waffle batter by whisking eggs in a bowl. Add milk and sunflower oil, whisking to combine. Sift 2 cups (500 mL) of flour, baking powder, and ¼ tsp (1 mL) of salt into milk-egg mixture, stirring to combine. Add the Candied Bacon bits and combine without overworking the batter. Set aside at room temperature.

In a heavy-bottomed pot, heat canola oil to 350°F (180°C).

Preheat a waffle iron.

In a large bowl, combine remaining 3 cups (750 mL) of flour, star anise, cinnamon, ginger, 1 Tbsp (15 mL) of salt, and pepper. Mix well, and set aside at room temperature.

Working with one chicken thigh at a time, transfer chicken from the Master Stock to the flour mixture. Coat well, ensuring a complete coating of flour mixture on chicken. Place floured chicken in the hot oil, and repeat this process until all chicken is in the fryer. Cook for 8 to 10 minutes or until chicken is crispy, golden brown, and cooked through.

Follow the directions for storing the Master Stock in the Master Stock recipe.

While chicken is frying, pour waffle batter into waffle iron and cook according to manufacturer's directions. Repeat until all waffle batter is cooked. Set aside at room temperature.

When chicken is done, remove from the pot and place on paper towel to absorb excess oil.

To serve, place equal portions of waffles in a neat stack on serving plates, and place two pieces of fried chicken on top. Liberally dress with Toasted Coconut Cream and Chili Caramel. Garnish with cilantro and serve immediately.

→ SERVES 4 ←

RAS EL HANOUT BRAISED CHICKEN WITH FRAGRANT COUSCOUS

CHICKEN

2 Tbsp (30 mL) canola oil, divided

8 bone-in, skinless chicken thighs

16 cipollini onions, peeled

1 large yellow onion, finely diced

4 cloves garlic, finely chopped

¼ cup (60 mL) Ras El Hanout (page 238)

2 cups (500 mL) canned crushed tomatoes

5⅔ cups (1.4 L) water, divided

1 cup (250 mL) green olives, unpitted

kosher salt, to taste

black pepper, freshly cracked, to taste

COUSCOUS

2 cups (500 mL) couscous

2 Tbsp (30 mL) sunflower oil, divided

5 Tbsp (75 mL) unsalted butter

½ tsp (2 mL) ground cinnamon

½ tsp (2 mL) ground allspice

½ tsp (2 mL) ground ginger

½ tsp (2 mL) ground cardamom

½ tsp (2 mL) ground coriander seeds

½ tsp (2 mL) ground cumin

1½ cups (375 mL) cilantro leaves, divided

½ cup (125 mL) dill fronds

1 Tbsp (15 mL) Harissa
  (page 231)

zest of 1 Preserved Lemons (page 248),
  finely diced

This dish calls for preserved lemon, which must be made ahead of time as per the recipe on page 248. If you do not have time to preserve lemons, you can substitute fresh lemon zest.

This Moroccan braised chicken stew is one of my favourite tagines. The rich, spicy, and earthy flavours from the Ras El Hanout permeate the stewed chicken meat, and the fragrant couscous provides a fresh balance of texture and flavour.

Cipollini onions are small, flat onions. Their flat shape allows for an even roast, and they are higher in residual sugar than other onions, but don't contain as much residual sugar as red shallots. If you can't find cipollini onions at your market, you can substitute red shallots.

Ideally, this dish should be plated in traditional clay tagines, but can be served in ornamental or decorative tagines as well. You can find traditional clay cooking tagines at Middle Eastern grocers or online from specialty retailers.

TO PREPARE THE CHICKEN, in a large, heavy-bottomed skillet, heat 1 Tbsp (15 mL) of canola oil over high heat. Add chicken and cook for 5 minutes or until evenly browned on all sides. Transfer chicken to paper towel to absorb excess oil. Add cipollini onions to the hot skillet, and cook for 5 minutes or until browned on all sides. Once cooked, set onions aside at room temperature with the chicken.

In a large pot, heat 1 Tbsp (15 mL) of canola oil over high heat. Sweat yellow onion and garlic for approximately 3 minutes. Add Ras El Hanout, and stir to combine. Cook for approximately 2 minutes, stirring occasionally. Add tomatoes, and stir to combine. Add 4 cups (1 L) of water, and stir to distribute ingredients. Add the browned chicken and olives. Bring to a boil, and then reduce heat to medium and braise chicken for 45 minutes or until chicken is tender and falling from the bone. Season with salt and pepper.

TO PREPARE THE COUSCOUS, place couscous in a bowl. Add half of the remaining cold water, just under 1 cup (200 mL), to the couscous. Using a carving fork and your hands, work to combine the water and the couscous, breaking up any lumps. Let stand for approximately 10 minutes. After 10 minutes, add the remaining cold water and 1 Tbsp (15 mL) of sunflower oil. Using a carving fork and your hands, stir to combine. Gently rub couscous between your hands to break up any lumps. Allow to stand for an additional 10 minutes. After 10 minutes, use your hands to break up the couscous.

Set up a steamer and bring to a boil. Cut muslin cloth to fit the steamer basket(s) with some cloth slightly overhanging. Wet cheesecloth with cold water and lightly squeeze out excess water. Place cloth in the steamer, covering the basket bottoms. Add couscous, and spread out to form an even, thin layer. Fold the excess muslin cloth over top of the couscous. Steam for 10 minutes. Remove steamer from heat.

Carefully transfer the couscous to a bowl. Add butter, and use a large serving fork to work it into the couscous. Add the dried spices, and combine. As the couscous cools to a manageable temperature, use your hands to finish off the mixing, breaking up any lumps. Season with salt to taste. Finely chop ½ cup (125 mL) of cilantro and add to the couscous, gently tossing to combine.

To serve, place equal portions of couscous in a pyramid shape in the base of serving tagines. Place 2 chicken thighs neatly to the side of the couscous in each tagine. Spoon tomato sauce, cooked cipollini onions, and olives over top of the couscous and around the edges of the tagines.

In a small bowl, combine the dill, remaining cilantro, Harissa, and 1 Tbsp (15 mL) of sunflower oil. Garnish the tagine with the herb mixture and Preserved Lemon zest. Serve immediately.

→ SERVES 4 ←

When we first opened the truck, we didn't have many fish and seafood dishes. But with the help of our friends at The Tide and Vine Oyster Company, who are our seafood suppliers, we've been able to introduce a lot more seafood to the menu. Coming from Australia, I have a deep love for fresh seafood. With the help of Mike Langley from Tide & Vine, we've been able to source some incredible products from the ocean.

One of my favourite foods in the world is octopus. When we first put an octopus dish on the truck menu there were a lot of naysayers who said people would never buy it. All it took was a little gentle nudging and some free samples to sway the non-believers. Now the octopus has become a hot commodity from the truck window, and we've noticed it popping up on other food truck menus over the last year. Whether it be pickled or grilled, our customers can't get enough of it.

Ceviche is a long-standing menu item on the streets of Peru, and it has made its way onto North American trucks in recent years. Unfortunately, with the preconception that food trucks were unsanitary, the running joke was "Why would you order ceviche off a food truck? Do you want to die?" Fortunately, that prejudice has changed, and with the rise of the modern food truck, which is held to the same strict standards as restaurants in terms of food safety and refrigeration, ceviche has become a popular menu item among North American street-food vendors.

FISH

CARPACCIO OF SALMON, TUNA, AND
SCALLOPS **125**

DILL-CURED SALMON WITH POTATO
BLINIS **126**

PHETCHABURI FISH CAKES **129**

SALMON AVOCADO CEVICHE WITH
PICKLED GINGER AIOLI **130**

SALMON KIBBEH WITH CANDIED
BACON **131**

SMOKED TROUT CROQUETTES WITH
EGGPLANT RELISH **132**

SMOKED COD CHEEK AND JICAMA
SALAD **134**

TUNA KIBBEH NAYEH **135**

TUNISIAN BRIK WITH SALMON AND
SCALLOP **137**

TUNA RICE-PAPER ROLLS **140**

WHOLE TROUT CEVICHE WITH
AVOCADO AND SHALLOTS **141**

SEAFOOD

BOSTON LAGER STEAMED MUSSELS
WITH FRIES AND AIOLI **142**

CHICKPEA-BATTERED OYSTERS WITH
CELERIAC AND DUKKAH SALAD **145**

CRAB CAKES WITH APPLE AND
DUKKAH SALAD **147**

CHERMOULA PRAWNS WITH
MARINATED PEPPER SALAD **149**

CRAB SPRING ROLLS WITH ZHOUG **151**

PRAWN SIU MAI **154**

CRISPY SOFT-SHELL CRAB WITH PINE
NUT SKORDALIA **156**

CUMIN FRIED CALAMARI WITH
AIOLI **159**

MADRAS CURRIED SCALLOP AND
SALMON CEVICHE **161**

GRILLED OCTOPUS WITH POTATOES
AND CHIPOTLE GASTRIQUE **163**

PICKLED OCTOPUS WITH MARINATED
POTATO SALAD **166**

OYSTERS À LA GRECQUE **169**

SCALLOP AND COCONUT MILK
CEVICHE **171**

SCALLOP AND ZHOUG CEVICHE **172**

SCALLOP AND CURRIED CORN
CEVICHE **172**

CARPACCIO OF SALMON, TUNA, AND SCALLOPS

2 bird's eye chilies, seeded and
  finely chopped
1 small red shallot, finely diced
1 small clove garlic, finely chopped
½-inch (1 cm) long piece ginger, peeled
  and finely chopped
1 Tbsp (15 mL) cilantro leaves,
  finely chopped
6 large fresh scallops
7 oz (200 g) sashimi-grade tuna, very
  finely sliced
7 oz (200 g) sashimi-grade salmon, very
  finely sliced
1 batch Ponzu (recipe follows)
1 Tbsp (15 mL) sesame oil
¼ cup (60 mL) sunflower shoots
2 Tbsp (30 mL) bonito flakes

> Bonito flakes are available at
> most Asian grocers.
>
> Ask your fishmonger to slice or
> shave the sashimi-grade tuna
> and salmon very finely, just as
> they would for smoked salmon.

This dish is inspired by a similar plate served by Chef Tony Sassi of Sassi Cucina e Bar in Port Douglas, Australia. A former Melbourne chef, Tony is as Italian as they come, but has a true love for Japanese food. He teamed up with chefs from Japan to have a sushi and raw bar at his restaurant.

I worked for Tony for a year in Port Douglas, and was lucky enough to learn a lot about seafood, with the amazing bounty and selection of fish we had at our disposal. Tony's version of this dish featured coral trout, tuna, and salmon, but the rest of the dish was always top secret. This is my take on it.

Place a large, flat serving platter into the refrigerator to cool for at least 30 minutes prior to preparing carpaccio.

In a small bowl, combine chilies, shallot, garlic, ginger, and cilantro. Mix well.

On a cool, clean cutting surface, turn the scallops on their sides and slice them into very fine disks.

 Wearing gloves while doing this is ideal.

Over the surface of the chilled serving platter, carefully arrange slices of tuna, scallops, and salmon in a mosaic pattern. Pour all of the Ponzu evenly over the entire surface of the seafood and platter. Evenly sprinkle the seafood with the chili-shallot mixture and lightly dress with sesame oil. Sporadically garnish with sunflower shoots and bonito flakes. Serve immediately.

 I like to enjoy this dish family-style.

⇒ SERVES 4 ⇐

PONZU

2 Tbsp (30 mL) light soy sauce
¼ cup (60 mL) lemon juice,
  freshly squeezed
1 Tbsp (15 mL) rice vinegar

In a small bowl, combine all ingredients, and mix well.

Use immediately or transfer to an airtight container and store in the refrigerator for up to 3 months.

⇒ MAKES ½ CUP (125 ML) ⇐

PHETCHABURI FISH CAKES

1 lb (500 g) firm-fleshed white fish (such as snapper, mackerel, or kingfish)

2 egg whites

1 Tbsp (15 mL) Green Curry Paste (page 258)

1 Tbsp (15 mL) fish sauce, more if needed

1 Tbsp (15 mL) palm sugar, grated

3 cups (750 mL) Thai basil leaves, divided

5 snake beans (Chinese long beans), roughly sliced

4 cups (1 L) canola oil

7 oz (200 g) dried vermicelli noodles

½ English cucumber

1 cup (250 mL) Chili Caramel (page 265)

> Snake beans are also called Chinese long beans and are available at most Asian grocery stores.

Phetchaburi is a province in central Thailand, known for its fish cakes served as street food and in restaurants. These fresh and aromatic fish cakes are extremely addictive, and fun to eat when served as a traditional street food in a plastic bag.

Cut fish into small pieces suitable for a food processor. Place fish, egg whites, Green Curry Paste, fish sauce, and palm sugar into a food processor. Purée until smooth. Transfer contents to a large bowl.

Roughly tear three-quarters of the basil, and add to the fish mixture with snake beans. Combine thoroughly and set aside in the refrigerator.

In a large, heavy-bottomed pot, heat oil to 350°F (180°C).

In a deep container or bowl, place noodles, and cover completely with boiling water. Allow noodles to reconstitute for 5 minutes or until tender but not falling apart. Carefully strain soaked noodles through a colander, and rinse gently under cold running water to remove excess starch. Place rinsed noodles in a bowl, and set aside at room temperature.

Cut cucumber in half crosswise, and then cut each half lengthwise. Slice pieces into long sticks. Set aside at room temperature.

Carefully spoon tablespoon-sized portions of the fish mixture into the hot oil, and deep-fry for 2 to 3 minutes or until golden brown. Remove from the pot and place on paper towel to absorb excess oil.

In a large bowl, combine noodles and Chili Caramel. Gently toss.

To serve, place equal portions of noodles into 4 serving bowls. Top noodles with equal portions of fish cakes and cucumber sticks, and garnish with remaining basil. Serve immediately.

→→ SERVES 4 ←←

SALMON AVOCADO CEVICHE WITH PICKLED GINGER AIOLI

½ cup (125 mL) Japanese pickled ginger,
   finely chopped
½ cup (125 mL) Mayonnaise (page 266)
1 large ripe avocado
1¼ lb (625 g) sashimi-grade
   boneless, skinless salmon
juice of 3 limes
¼ cup (60 mL) wasabi *tobiko*
½ cup (125 mL) sunflower shoots
1 Tbsp (15 mL) sunflower oil

Pickled ginger and wasabi *tobiko* are available at most Asian or Japanese grocers and some specialty seafood suppliers.

In this ceviche, the pickled ginger and wasabi *tobiko* (flying fish roe flavoured with wasabi) bring a very Japanese flavour profile to a Peruvian street-food classic. If you cannot find wasabi *tobiko*, you can substitute it with any other flavoured *tobiko* or, alternatively, salmon roe.

In a small bowl, combine pickled ginger and Mayonnaise. Gently mix, and set aside in the refrigerator.

Peel and remove the pit from the avocado. Cut avocado flesh into ½-inch (1 cm) cubes. Set aside.

Wearing gloves, cut salmon into ½-inch (1 cm) cubes on a cool, clean cutting surface. Place salmon cubes in a small bowl. Cover with lime juice and mix to coat well. Allow salmon to marinate in lime juice for 2 to 4 minutes, stirring once. Add avocado cubes, and mix gently to combine.

Using a slotted spoon, place equal amounts of salmon-avocado mixture onto serving plates. Using a small spoon, stud salmon mixture with pickled ginger aioli. Sprinkle wasabi *tobiko* over salmon. Garnish with sunflower shoots and lightly dress with oil. Serve immediately.

→ SERVES 4 ←

SALMON KIBBEH WITH CANDIED BACON

¼ cup (60 mL) bulgur (bulgur wheat)

¼ cup (60 mL) cilantro leaves, finely chopped

¼ cup (60 mL) flat leaf parsley leaves, finely chopped

¼ cup (60 mL) mint leaves, finely chopped

¾ lb (375 g) boneless, skinless salmon

1 Tbsp (15 mL) sunflower oil

1 green onion, finely sliced

1 tsp (5 mL) ground allspice

3 oz (90 g) Candied Bacon, finely chopped (page 249)

kosher salt, to taste

black pepper, freshly cracked, to taste

½ cup (125 mL) Labne (page 270)

1 cup (250 mL) whole tarragon leaves

juice from ½ lemon

4 cups (1 L) canola oil

This is a very loose play on the cooked version of kibbeh, which is traditionally a fried lamb snack. My version is a salmon rissole, seared on the grill rather than deep-fried.

Place bulgur in a small bowl and add enough cold water to just cover. Set aside at room temperature until bulgur soaks up all of the water, and fluff with a fork to separate grains. Taste a small amount of bulgur, and if the grains are still nutty, repeat the soaking and fluffing process until there is no nutty taste. Soaking time can vary depending on the grain, but can take approximately 30 minutes.

Using a meat grinder, grind salmon on largest setting. If you do not have a meat grinder, mince the salmon with a sharp knife without turning the salmon to a mush. Place ground salmon into a small bowl. Add soaked bulgur, sunflower oil, chopped herbs, green onion, allspice, and Candied Bacon. Season with salt and pepper and mix gently but thoroughly, and set aside in the refrigerator until ready to cook.

Place Labne in a small bowl. Chop tarragon and combine with Labne. Season with lemon juice and mix thoroughly.

In a heavy-bottomed pot, heat canola oil to 350°F (180°C).

Wearing gloves, form approximately ¼ cup (60 mL) of salmon mixture into a rounded conical shape with a flat bottom. Repeat until all salmon mixture has been used. Deep-fry for 3 minutes or until golden brown. Remove from pot and place on paper towel to absorb excess oil.

To serve, push Labne in a line across each serving plate. Sit kibbehs pointy-end-up in a row down the middle of the Labne. Serve immediately.

→→ SERVES 4 ←←

SMOKED TROUT CROQUETTES WITH EGGPLANT RELISH

3 large Yukon gold potatoes, peeled

1 2 lb (1 kg) whole smoked trout, meat picked
  from bones

4 cups (1 L) all-purpose flour
  (approx.), divided

1 tsp (5 mL) kosher salt

½ tsp (2 mL) freshly cracked black pepper

4 cups (1 L) canola oil

½ cup (125 mL) flat leaf parsley leaves

½ cup (125 mL) cilantro leaves

1 large red shallot, finely sliced

juice of 1 lemon

½ cup (125 mL) Eggplant and Pomegranate
  Relish (recipe follows)

You can find smoked trout at any good delicatessen or specialty seafood supplier. Smoked trout, as opposed to salt cod (*bacalao*), adds an interesting flavour profile to these croquettes. The tangy Eggplant and Pomegranate Relish cuts through the creamy, smoky flavour of the croquettes.

Cut potatoes into quarters, place in a pot with enough water to cover potatoes, and bring to a boil over high heat. Reduce heat, and simmer for 20 minutes or until fork-tender.

Once cooked, strain potatoes and transfer to a medium bowl. Mash until smooth. Add smoked trout meat, 1 cup (250 mL) of flour, salt, and pepper. Gently combine mixture, being careful not to overwork. Add up to 1 cup (250 mL) more flour, if necessary, until the mixture holds its shape without being too wet. Set aside at room temperature, if using immediately.

 If making ahead of time, you can cover mixture and store in the refrigerator for up to 24 hours.

In a medium heavy-bottomed pot, heat oil to 350°F (180°C).

Using two dessert spoons, shape croquette mixture into egg-shaped portions (cornels). Lightly dredge cornels in flour, and deep-fry for 2 minutes or until golden brown. Remove from pot and place on paper towel to absorb excess oil.

Make an herb salad, combining parsley, cilantro, and shallot in a small bowl. Dress with lemon juice, and lightly season with salt. Set aside.

Neatly arrange croquettes on a serving plate. Serve with Eggplant and Pomegranate Relish and herb salad on the side.

↠ SERVES 4 ↞

EGGPLANT AND POMEGRANATE RELISH

1 eggplant
1 small red onion, finely diced
¼ cup (60 mL) pomegranate molasses
kosher salt, to taste
black pepper, freshly cracked, to taste

Pomegranate molasses can be found at Middle Eastern and specialty grocery stores.

Preheat grill or barbecue to highest temperature.

Using a small paring knife, prick eggplant skin all over. Place whole eggplant on grill and cook for 15 minutes or until skin is scorched, rotating until eggplant is charred on all sides. Alternatively, you can hold the pricked eggplant with heat-proof tongs over an open flame on a gas range until the eggplant is charred on all sides. Remove the charred eggplant from heat and allow to cool.

Very carefully remove the stem and as much of the charred eggplant skin as possible, leaving only the flesh. Finely chop the eggplant, and place in a small bowl with onion and pomegranate molasses. Combine thoroughly and season with salt and pepper.

Use immediately or transfer to an airtight container and store in the refrigerator for up to 1 week.

→→ MAKES ¾ CUP (185 ML) ←←

TUNISIAN BRIK WITH SALMON AND SCALLOP

1 small celeriac, peeled and cut into
 ½-inch (1 cm) cubes

1 Tbsp (15 mL) unsalted butter

1 cup (250 mL) water

juice of 1 lemon

kosher salt, to taste

black pepper, freshly cracked, to taste

7 oz (200 g) salmon, skin on, deboned

4 sheets *brik* pastry

4 large fresh scallops

½ fennel bulb, finely shaved

¼ cup (60 mL) dill fronds

¼ cup (60 mL) cilantro leaves

¼ cup (60 mL) flat leaf parsley leaves

1 red shallot, finely sliced

1 tsp (5 mL) sumac

juice of 1 lime

½ lemon, quartered

> You will need 4 metal ring moulds, approximately 3 inches (8 cm) in diameter and at least 1½ inches (4 cm) in height.

Tunisian *brik* refers to a filled pastry that is either baked or deep-fried. Traditionally, a specific *brik* pastry (*malsouka* or *warka*) is used, which can be found at Middle Eastern grocery stores. In North America, phyllo pastry is easier to find, and can be used as a substitute. If using phyllo pastry, cut sheets in half to form two squares; using melted butter, glue together four sheets of phyllo to create the equivalent of one sheet of *brik* pastry.

In a small pot, bring celeriac, butter, and water to a boil over high heat. Cover with a lid and reduce heat to medium-low. Simmer gently for 20 minutes or until celeriac is completely softened. Remove from heat and allow to cool slightly. Empty the entire contents of the pot into a blender, and purée until smooth. Transfer purée into a small bowl, and add lemon juice, stirring to combine. Season with salt and pepper. Set aside at room temperature and allow to cool completely. Celeriac mixture should be firm but moist once cooled.

Preheat oven to 300°F (150°C).

Place salmon, skin side down, on a baking sheet lined with parchment paper. Place baking sheet in oven, and cook salmon for 15 minutes or until medium-well done. Remove from oven, and allow salmon to cool slightly at room temperature.

Wearing gloves, remove skin from salmon and discard. Gently flake salmon flesh into a small bowl and lightly season with salt and pepper. Set flaked salmon aside to cool completely.

Preheat oven to 350°F (180°C).

Using your finger, lightly grease the inside of the ring moulds with oil. Tuck the centre of one sheet of *brik* pastry into a ring mould, leaving remaining pastry overlapping the edge of each mould. Working in layers, place a scallop in the centre of the ring mould. Carefully spoon celeriac purée around the scallop, with a small amount on top of the scallop. Add a layer of flaked salmon, followed by another layer of celeriac purée. Gently fold the *brik* pastry edges over the top of the filling, tucking pastry in to completely enclose the filling. Repeat this process with each of the ring moulds.

Continued on next page

Continued from previous page

Lightly oil a small baking sheet, and place filled ring moulds on the sheet, folded side up. Place in the oven, and bake for 12 to 15 minutes, flipping *briks* once halfway through the baking time. *Briks* should be golden brown on top. Remove from oven, and set aside at room temperature.

In a small bowl, combine fennel, herbs, shallot, and sumac. Mix gently. Set aside at room temperature.

To serve, remove ring moulds from *briks*. Using a thin metal spatula, transfer each *brik* to a serving plate, folded side down. Dress mixed fennel salad with lime juice, gently tossing to combine. Using one hand, separate 4 equal portions of salad. Twist each portion into a neat salad ball, and place 1 portion of salad on top of each *brik*. Serve immediately with a lemon wedge.

→→ SERVES 4 ←←

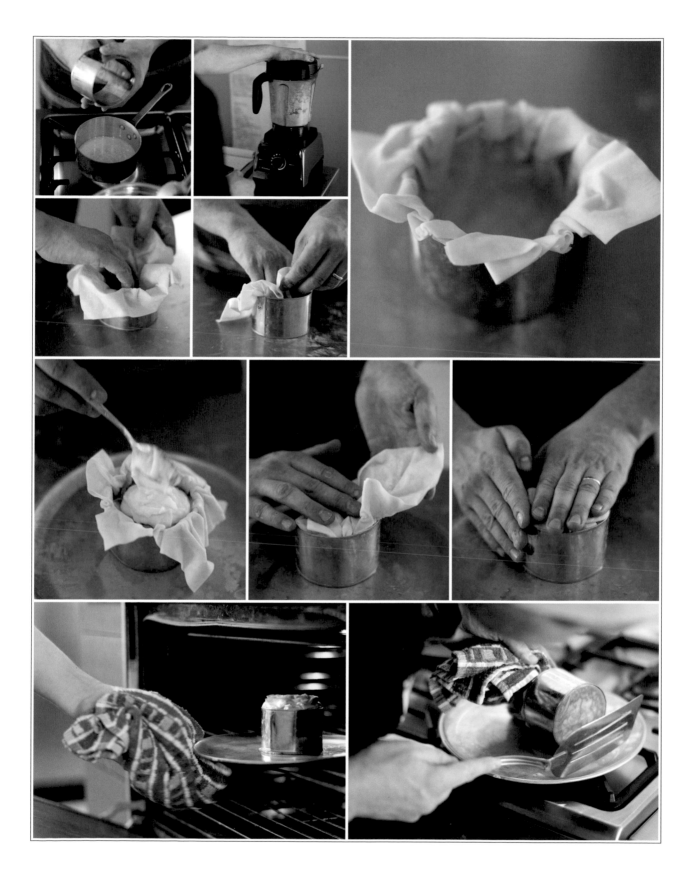

BOSTON LAGER STEAMED MUSSELS WITH FRIES AND AIOLI

8 large russet potatoes

8 cups (2 L) + 1 Tbsp (30 mL) canola oil

48 large mussels

1 small red onion, finely sliced

2 cups (500 mL) Samuel Adams
   Boston Lager

2 cups (500 mL) water

2 Roma tomatoes

¼ cup (60 mL) Wet Chermoula (page 234)

¼ cup (60 mL) heavy cream (approx.)

kosher salt, to taste

black pepper, freshly cracked, to taste

½ cup (125 mL) cilantro leaves

1 lemon, quartered

1 cup (250 mL) Smoked Tomato Aioli
   (page 272)

> Cooking fries is a two-step process. The first step will be to blanch the fries, and the second is to fry just before serving.

The Boston Beer Company, the makers of Samuel Adams, have been an avid supporter of food trucks and the growing street-food scene in Ontario and beyond. This recipe features the Boston Lager, which is the perfect beer for cooking mussels. Its smooth and velvety finish and spicy character makes for a balanced sauce. If you don't have access to this particular beer, I recommend a light lager with a similar flavour profile.

Mussels and fries have always been a popular snack to accompany beer, whether it be in a restaurant, beer garden, or al fresco dining on the street.

Rinse potatoes under cold running water, and let soak in a bowl for a minimum of 1 hour.

Using a sharp knife, hand-cut fries lengthwise, ½ inch (1 cm) in width. Fill a clean sink basin or very large bowl with cold water, and submerge cut fries, rinsing off any excess starch. Transfer fries to paper towel to absorb excess moisture. Pat dry with paper towel to remove additional moisture, and set aside at room temperature.

In a large, heavy-bottomed pot, heat 8 cups (2 L) of oil to 350°F (180°C).

To cook the fries, work in batches, placing fries in hot oil and cooking for 5 minutes or until cooked through and soft, but not crispy. Using a spider or slotted spoon, remove fries from the pot and transfer to paper towel to absorb excess oil. Repeat this process until all fries are cooked. Set cooked fries aside at room temperature, reserving the oil. Turn off heat until ready to serve.

Heat water in a pot over high heat. Bring to a boil. Remove the core from two tomatoes, and score the skin on the opposite end with a paring knife. Place the tomatoes in boiling water, and count to 10. Turn off heat, carefully remove tomatoes from water and place them in a sieve. Rinse tomatoes under cold running water until chilled, approximately 2 minutes. Peel the skin from the chilled tomatoes, and cut in quarters lengthwise. Remove the seeds, and finely dice the tomatoes. Set aside.

Continued on next page

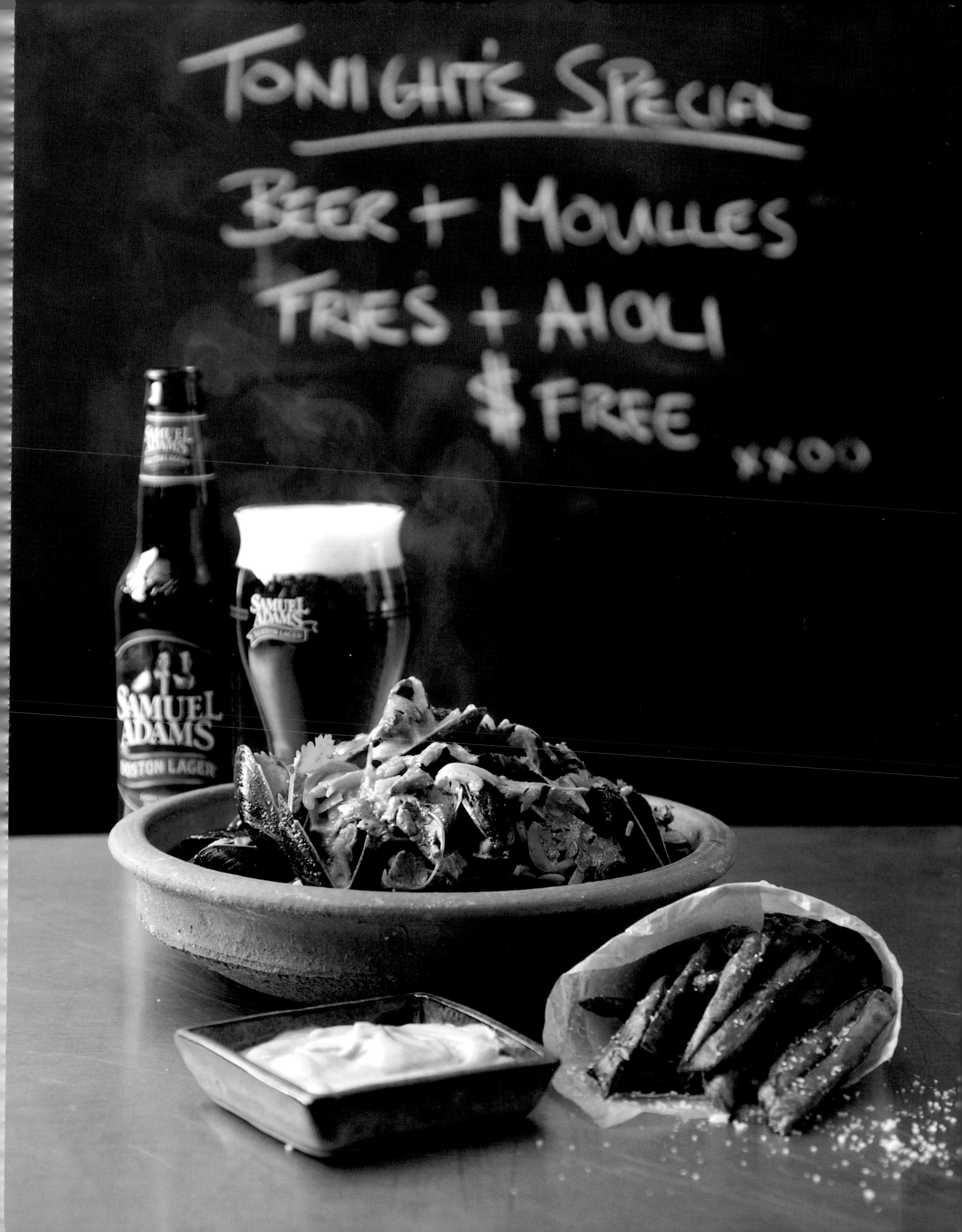

TONIGHT'S SPECIAL
BEER + MOULLES
FRIES + AIOLI
$ FREE
xxoo
SAMUEL ADAMS
BOSTON LAGER
SAMUEL ADAMS
BOSTON LAGER

CRAB CAKES WITH APPLE AND DUKKAH SALAD

1 whole live Dungeness crab or
  1 lb (500 g) crab meat

1 tsp (5 mL) + 2 Tbsp (30 mL)
  grape seed oil

4 red shallots, finely diced + 1 red shallot,
  finely shaved

1½-inches (4 cm) long piece ginger,
  peeled and finely diced

2 cloves garlic, minced

1 bird's eye chili, seeded and
  finely chopped

½ cup (125 mL) cilantro leaves,
  finely chopped

2 cups (500 mL) panko bread crumbs

1 egg, lightly beaten

kosher salt, to taste

black pepper, freshly cracked, to taste

¼ cup (60 mL) Mayonnaise (page 266)

1 Tbsp (15 mL) Harissa (page 231)

¼ tsp (1 mL) ground coriander

1 crisp Fuji or other sweet
  apple, unpeeled

1 red shallot, finely chopped

1 Tbsp (15 mL) Dukkah (page 237)

½ cup (125 mL) dill fronds

1 Tbsp (15 mL) olive oil

juice of ½ lemon

1 Tbsp (15 mL) sumac

Crab cakes are a popular and versatile dish made the world over. In this recipe, I pair the crab cakes with a spicy aioli and a sweet, sour, and earthy salad that brings the dish together. If you don't want to cook the crab yourself, you can find cooked crab meat at your local seafood supplier.

Fill a large pot three-quarters full with water. Bring water to a rapid boil over high heat. Carefully place the crab in boiling water and cook, covered, for 21 minutes. While crab is cooking, fill a large bowl with ice and water. Remove cooked crab from boiling water and submerge in ice bath. Allow crab to cool completely.

Remove crab from ice bath and discard water. Separate the crab legs and top shell from the body of the crab. Discard the top shell, the mustard (tomalley), and dead man's fingers or gills. Using a crab picking stick, carefully pick all of the crab meat from the body. Crack the shells on all legs and claws to remove crab meat. Discard all remaining shell and carefully pick through meat for unwanted shell fragments. Place meat in a bowl, and set aside.

In a small non-stick skillet, heat 1 tsp (5 mL) of grape seed oil on medium heat. Sweat diced shallots, ginger, garlic, and chili for 3 to 5 minutes or until translucent, stirring occasionally. Remove from heat, set aside at room temperature, and allow to cool.

In a medium bowl, combine cooled shallot mixture and crab. Add cilantro, panko, and egg. Using your hands, combine well. Season mixture with salt and pepper.

 The crab mixture should hold its shape. If too wet, add more panko bread crumbs or if too dry, add another egg.

Divide crab mixture into small portions, approximately 2 Tbsp (30 mL) each, and form portions into tiny pucks. Place pucks onto a plate and place in the refrigerator.

 Extra crab cakes can be stored in the refrigerator for up to 3 days.

Continued on next page

CRAB SPRING ROLLS WITH ZHOUG

1 whole live Dungeness crab or
   1 lb (500 g) crab meat
½ cup (125 mL) cilantro leaves,
   finely chopped
4 red shallots, finely diced
2 cloves garlic, minced
2 bird's eye chilies, seeded and
   finely chopped
½ cup (125 mL) Dukkah (page 237)
2 eggs, divided
1 cup (250 mL) panko bread crumbs
1 tsp (5 mL) kosher salt (approx.)
½ tsp (2 mL) freshly cracked black pepper
   (approx.)
4 cups (1 L) canola oil
24 small spring roll wrappers
1 batch Zhoug (page 274)

If you don't want to cook the crab yourself, you can find cooked crab meat at your local seafood supplier.

Spring roll wrappers can be found at most Asian grocers. If you cannot find small ones (approximately 4 inches / 10 cm square) you can use 6 large wrappers and cut them into quarters.

These light, crisp crab spring rolls are a perfect finger food for a cocktail party. Zhoug adds a spicy, zesty kick to the sweet crab meat.

Fill a large pot three-quarters full with water. Bring water to a rapid boil over high heat. Carefully place the live crab in boiling water and cook, covered, for 21 minutes. While crab is cooking, fill a large bowl with ice and water. Remove cooked crab from boiling water and submerge in ice bath. Allow crab to cool completely.

Remove crab from ice bath and discard water. Separate the crab legs and top shell from the body of the crab. Discard the top shell, the mustard (tomalley), and dead man's fingers or gills. Using a crab picking stick, carefully pick all of the crab meat from the body. Crack the shells on all legs and claws to remove crab meat. Discard all remaining shell, and carefully pick through meat for unwanted shell fragments. Place meat in a bowl, and set aside in the refrigerator.

In a medium bowl, combine cilantro, shallots, garlic, chilies, Dukkah, 1 egg, panko, crab meat, salt, and pepper. Combine well. Season to taste with additional salt and pepper, if needed. Set aside in the refrigerator.

In a small bowl, whisk remaining 1 egg with a fork, and set aside at room temperature.

Carefully lay out 4 spring roll wrappers on a clean work surface. Spoon a manageable amount, approximately 1 Tbsp (15 mL), of crab mixture onto the bottom third of the wrapper, leaving at least ½ inch (1 cm) of space along the edge of the wrapper on the left and right sides, and the bottom.

Using your finger or a very small pastry brush, lightly paint a small line of egg wash along the left and right edges of the wrapper. Fold the left and right edges over the mixture, pressing the edges down to form a neat seam along the length of the wrapper.

Fold the bottom edge of the wrapper over the mixture, and gently but firmly roll the spring roll, leaving ½ inch (1 cm) of wrapper exposed at the top. Lightly wash the top edge of the wrapper with egg wash and finish rolling the wrapper. Press gently but firmly to seal the spring roll.

Continued on next page

Continued from previous page

Repeat this process with the remaining spring roll wrappers until all of the crab mixture has been used.

 Spring rolls can be frozen at this point to be cooked later or can be cooked immediately.

In a medium pot, heat oil to 350°F (180°C).

Carefully deep-fry spring rolls in hot oil for 2 minutes or until golden brown and crispy. Remove from pot and place on paper towel to absorb excess oil.

Serve crab spring rolls with Zhoug on the side.

→ SERVES 4 ←

PRAWN SIU MAI

1 Tbsp (15 mL) canola oil

2-inches (5 cm) long piece ginger, peeled and finely diced

5 red shallots, finely diced

24 large prawns, peeled and deveined, heads and tails removed

8 water chestnuts, peeled and finely diced

1 Tbsp (15 mL) sesame oil

4 green onions, finely sliced

2 Tbsp (30 mL) soy sauce (approx.)

1 egg white

¼ cup (60 mL) cornstarch (approx.)

32 small square wonton wrappers

¾ cup (185 mL) Chinese red vinegar

½ cup (125 mL) Sriracha

> Wonton wrappers and Chinese red vinegar are available at most Asian grocers.
>
> Chinese red vinegar gets its colour from red rice yeast, and has a distinctive sweet and tangy flavour.

Siu mai are Chinese steamed dumplings that traditionally contain pork, prawns, chicken, or a combination of these. If you are setting out to make these dumplings, you might want to multiply the recipe and make a larger batch for freezing and cooking later. These dumplings are popular at hawkers markets in Asia and Chinatowns around the world.

In a pan, heat canola oil over medium-high heat. Sweat the ginger and shallots for 5 minutes or until translucent, stirring occasionally to prevent catching. Remove from heat and allow to cool completely at room temperature.

Cut prawns in half lengthwise and place in a medium bowl with cooled ginger and shallots. Place contents of bowl in a resealable bag, and allow to marinate in the refrigerator for a minimum of 12 hours or overnight.

Place marinated prawn mixture on a chopping board, and using two knives, roughly chop mixture with a drumming motion. Do not finely chop.

In a bowl, combine chopped prawn mixture, water chestnuts, sesame oil, green onions, soy sauce, and egg white. Mix well. Add cornstarch, and combine further. Set aside in the refrigerator.

In a small pan, place a small spoonful of the prawn mixture and cook over medium-high heat for 2 minutes or until cooked through to test for seasoning. Taste and add more soy sauce if needed.

On a clean, dry work surface, spread out wonton wrappers so they are not touching. Carefully spoon approximately 1 Tbsp (15 mL) of the prawn mixture into the centre of each wrapper. Using a spray bottle filled with cold water, lightly mist the surface of the wonton wrappers. Working one dumpling at time, bring the opposing corners of each wrapper up the sides of the filling, and repeat with the other corners. Leave the top of the *siu mai* open, and tuck the remaining edges of the wrapper into one another to enclose the sides of the *siu mai*. Repeat this process with the remaining wrappers. Place formed *siu mai* on a tray lined with parchment paper, and place in the refrigerator.

Fill the basin of a steamer or a pot that fits a bamboo steamer basket with approximately 2 inches (5 cm) of hot water. Heat water to a rapid boil over high heat, and cook *siu mai* in the steamer basket for 3 to 5 minutes or until cooked through. Place vinegar and Sriracha in separate small sauce bowls for dipping. Serve with *siu mai* while hot.

→→ SERVES 4 ←←

CRISPY SOFT-SHELL CRAB WITH PINE NUT SKORDALIA

2 soft-shell crabs

2 cups (500 mL) self-rising flour

1 cup (250 mL) soda water (approx.)

1 cup (250 mL) all-purpose flour

4 cups (1 L) canola oil

1 crisp Fuji or other sweet apple

½ fennel bulb, finely shaved

½ cup (125 mL) dill fronds

2 Tbsp (30 mL) Za'atar (page 238)

1 red shallot, finely shaved

½ cup (125 mL) Pine Nut Skordalia (page 271)

1 Tbsp (15 mL) olive oil

juice of ½ lemon

This dish is best served when soft-shell crabs are in season and can be sourced fresh from your fish market or specialty seafood supplier. Out of season, you will only find them frozen. Soft-shell crabs, or blue crabs, are eaten whole, shell and all, although a little bit of cleaning and trimming is required.

Working one side at a time, carefully lift the outer edge of the top shell away from the crab until you can remove the crab gills (also called dead man's fingers). Repeat on the other side. Flip the crab over and pull the crab's apron (the flap covering the rear belly of the crab) until you can cut it off cleanly. Using kitchen shears or sharp, clean scissors, cut the eyes and mouth off of the crab. Discard the gills, apron, and mouth and eyes. Repeat this process with the second crab.

Using a sharp knife, cut each crab in half down the centre of the body from head to tail. Place crabs on paper towel to absorb excess moisture, and set aside in the refrigerator.

Place self-rising flour in a small bowl and create a well in the centre. While whisking, slowly add soda water until batter reaches a thin, smooth consistency, similar to that of crepe batter.

Place all-purpose flour in a separate small bowl for dredging.

In a large pot, heat canola oil to 350°F (180°C).

Just prior to serving, gently dredge each crab half in all-purpose flour, and submerge in batter. Draining off excess batter, carefully lower 2 crab pieces into hot oil. Deep-fry for 3 to 4 minutes or until golden brown, crisp, and cooked. Remove crab from pot and place on paper towel to absorb excess oil. Repeat this process with the remaining 2 crab pieces.

To decrease the chances of the apple flesh turning brown, prepare the apple salad as close to serving time as possible. Working from the edge of the apple, with the peel still on, use a very sharp knife or mandolin to slice 1/32-inch (1 mm) thick slices, avoiding the core and seeds, until all four sides of the apple have been sliced. Working with a couple of slices at a time, finely julienne the apple and place into a bowl. Add fennel, dill fronds, Za'atar, and shallots and mix to combine. Set aside at room temperature.

Continued on next page

GRILLED OCTOPUS WITH POTATOES AND CHIPOTLE GASTRIQUE

2.2 lb (1 kg) whole frozen octopus, thawed and drained

16 new potatoes

1 Tbsp (15 mL) canola oil

1 tsp (5 mL) *fleur de sel*

1 batch Chipotle Gastrique (recipe follows)

1 tsp (5 mL) smoked paprika

1 Tbsp (15 mL) sunflower oil

¼ cup (60 mL) sunflower shoots

You will need butcher's twine for poaching the octopus.

Grilled octopus with potatoes is a classic Spanish dish, usually served in tapas bars. The potatoes get a subtle flavour from the octopus liquid, and then are dressed with the Chipotle Gastrique and paprika. I like to serve this combination to add a smoky, sweet, and sour balance to the dish.

This recipe explains how to cook a whole octopus. You can refer to the Pickled Octopus and Marinated Potato Salad recipe (page 166) for storage instructions for leftover cooked octopus.

Cut a piece of butcher's twine approximately 16 inches (40 cm) in length, and tie it tightly around the base of the head of the octopus, leaving excess twine attached. Holding the excess twine, carefully lower octopus into boiling water until fully submerged. Cook, continuing to boil, for approximately 15 seconds. Using the excess twine, remove octopus from boiling water and place in a bowl. Set aside at room temperature.

Allow pot of water to return to a boil and repeat this process three more times. On the fourth and final time submerging the octopus, leave it in the water and bring water back up to a simmer. Simmer for 45 minutes or until the octopus is tender.

 NOTE *To check tenderness, carefully remove a tentacle from the octopus and slice a small piece off of the thick end. The octopus should be wonderfully succulent and on the verge of falling apart in your mouth.*

Once cooked, carefully remove the octopus by the twine and place on a tray. The now-pink skin should still be intact. Be very careful not to damage the skin. Allow the octopus to cool to room temperature. Once cooled, place octopus, uncovered, on a tray in the refrigerator overnight.

In an ice bath, rapidly cool the octopus cooking liquid to room temperature, and refrigerate to cool completely.

On the day of serving, place potatoes in a medium pot and cover with reserved octopus cooking liquid. Bring to a boil over high heat. Once boiling, reduce heat to medium-high and simmer for 20 minutes or until tender. Strain potatoes, discarding cooking water, and allow to cool slightly. Cut potatoes into ¼-inch (6 mm) thick disks, place in a bowl, and set aside at room temperature.

Continued on next page

Continued from previous page

Carefully remove 2 octopus tentacles from the cooked octopus and cut each tentacle into ¼-inch (6 mm) thick disks. Place in a bowl and set aside.

In a heavy-bottomed skillet, heat canola oil over high heat. Carefully place octopus disks into the hot oil and fry on one side only for 2 minutes or until golden brown. Remove octopus from skillet and place on paper towel to absorb excess oil.

To serve, arrange potatoes in a mosaic pattern on serving plates. Lightly season with *fleur de sel*. Arrange octopus, golden side up, on top of potatoes, and lightly season with *fleur de sel*. Dress each plate liberally with Chipotle Gastrique, and dust with smoked paprika. Lightly dress with sunflower oil, and garnish with sunflower shoots. Serve immediately.

→→ SERVES 4 ←←

CHIPOTLE GASTRIQUE

1 cup (250 mL) palm sugar, shaved
¼ cup (60 mL) white vinegar
2 whole dried chipotle peppers
1 Tbsp (15 mL) water

In a small pot, combine all ingredients and bring to a boil over high heat. Stir to help dissolve palm sugar. Once boiling, reduce heat to medium, and simmer for 15 minutes or until liquid is reduced by one-quarter of its volume. Once reduced, remove from heat and allow to cool.

Use immediately or transfer to an airtight container and refrigerate for up to 3 months.

→→ MAKES ½ CUP (125 ML) ←←

PICKLED OCTOPUS WITH MARINATED POTATO SALAD

2.2 lb (1 kg) whole frozen octopus, thawed and drained

1 batch Pickling Liquid (recipe follows)

16 new potatoes

½ cup (125 mL) lemon juice

½ cup (125 mL) sunflower oil

1 tsp (5 mL) kosher salt

½ head broccoli, cut into small florets

¼ cup (60 mL) flat leaf parsley leaves

¼ cup (60 mL) cilantro leaves

black pepper, freshly cracked, to taste

¼ cup (60 mL) Aioli (page 266)

1 Tbsp (15 mL) sumac

¼ cup (60 mL) sunflower shoots

> You will need butcher's twine for poaching the octopus.

The recipe that follows explains how to pickle a whole octopus. Ideally, pickling should be done at least one week in advance of serving. When cooking for four people, two tentacles will be ample. The remaining tentacles can be stored covered in the pickling liquid in an airtight container in the refrigerator for up to three weeks. Alternatively, you can make this dish for up to 16 or more people using the whole octopus. Increase the other ingredients accordingly.

If you purchase your octopus fresh instead of frozen you will want to ensure you tenderize it. To tenderize the octopus, freeze it, whole, for at least three days, then thaw the octopus and drain excess liquid from it before using.

Fill a large pot three-quarters full with water. Bring water to a rapid boil over high heat.

Cut a piece of butcher's twine, approximately 16 inches (40 cm) in length, and tie it tightly around the base of the head of the octopus, leaving excess twine attached. Holding the excess twine, carefully lower octopus into boiling water until fully submerged. Cook, continuing to boil, for approximately 15 seconds. Using the excess twine, remove octopus from boiling water and place in a stainless steel bowl. Set aside at room temperature.

Allow pot of water to return to a boil and repeat this process three more times. On the fourth and final time submerging the octopus, leave it in the water and bring water back up to a simmer. Allow the octopus to simmer for 45 minutes or until the octopus is tender.

 To check tenderness, carefully remove a tentacle from the octopus and slice a small piece off the thick end. The octopus should be wonderfully succulent and on the verge of falling apart in your mouth.

Once cooked, carefully remove the octopus by the twine and place on a tray. The now-pink skin should still be intact. Be very careful not to damage the skin. Allow the octopus to cool to room temperature. Once cooled, place octopus, uncovered, on a tray and refrigerate overnight.

Continued on next page

SCALLOP AND COCONUT MILK CEVICHE

1 cup (250 mL) coconut milk

5 oz (150 g) tapioca pearls

12 fresh large scallops

juice of 6 limes

5 Tbsp (75 mL) Chili Caramel (approx.)
  (page 265)

¼ cup (60 mL) Fried Shallots (page 250)

1 large kaffir lime leaf, finely julienned

This ceviche is an example of simple flavours and textures coming together in harmony. The sweet tropical flavours are balanced with spice and sourness in this ceviche, and the tapioca pearls add a delightful textural touch to the scallops. This dish is a play on a Peruvian ceviche, using Asian flavours, and is very popular among our customers, with some travelling for two hours or more to get this dish when it is on the menu!

In a small pot, bring coconut milk to a simmer over medium-high heat. Do not allow coconut milk to boil. Remove from heat and allow to cool to room temperature. Transfer to an airtight container and place in the refrigerator to cool completely.

Fill a medium saucepan three-quarters full with water, and bring to a boil over high heat. Add tapioca pearls, stirring to prevent the pearls from sticking to the bottom of the pan. Reduce heat to medium, and simmer for 10 minutes or until pearls are almost completely transparent with a small speck of white in the centre of each pearl.

Strain tapioca through a fine sieve, discarding liquid. Rinse tapioca under cold running water until pearls are cool, and drain any excess liquid. Place tapioca into a small bowl and add cooled coconut milk. Mix well. Set aside in the refrigerator.

Wearing gloves, cut scallops into quarters on a cool, clean cutting surface. Place scallop meat in a bowl and cover with lime juice. Allow scallops to marinate in lime juice for approximately 4 minutes, stirring once. Add tapioca and coconut mixture to the scallop and lime bowl. Add Chili Caramel to this mixture, 1 Tbsp (15 mL) at a time, stirring gently to combine. Taste after each addition, until a balance of sweet, sour, and spicy has been achieved. Add more lime juice if necessary.

To serve, spoon equal amounts of ceviche into small chilled serving bowls. Garnish with Fried Shallots and lime leaf. Serve immediately.

→ SERVES 4 ←

SCALLOP AND ZHOUG CEVICHE

12 fresh large scallops

juice of 6 limes

¼ cup (60 mL) Zhoug (page 274)

1 avocado, cut into ½-inch (1 cm) cubes

¼ white onion, finely sliced

½ cup (125 mL) cilantro leaves

1 lime, quartered

This ceviche lets the scallops take centre stage, backed by the zesty kick of Zhoug. Onion and avocado add crunch and creaminess without stealing the show.

Wearing gloves, cut scallops into quarters on a cool, clean cutting surface. Place scallop meat in a bowl and cover with lime juice. Allow scallops to marinate in lime juice for approximately 4 minutes, stirring once.

In a separate bowl, combine Zhoug, avocado, and onion. Using a slotted spoon, remove scallops from lime juice and place in Zhoug mixture. Mix gently to combine.

To serve, spoon equal amounts of ceviche into 4 small chilled serving bowls. Garnish with cilantro and lime wedges. Serve immediately.

→ SERVES 4 ←

SCALLOP AND CURRIED CORN CEVICHE

½ cup (125 mL) coconut milk, divided

1 Tbsp (15 mL) Green Curry Paste (page 258)

kernels from 2 ears of corn

1 Tbsp (15 mL) palm sugar, shaved

1 tsp (5 mL) fish sauce (approx.)

12 fresh large scallops

juice of 6 limes

¼ white onion, finely sliced

¼ cup (60 mL) Fried Shallots (page 250)

1 large kaffir lime leaf, finely julienned

Both scallops and corn have a sweet, creamy flavour profile, which is brought to another level with the addition of a spicy, aromatic green curry paste in this ceviche. This ceviche is a unique way to celebrate the corn harvest on a hot late-summer day.

In a small pot, heat 1 Tbsp (15 mL) of coconut milk and Green Curry Paste for 2 to 3 minutes over high heat or until aromatic. Add corn and reduce heat to medium. Stir well. Add remaining coconut milk and simmer for 5 minutes or until corn is cooked.

Remove from heat, and add palm sugar and fish sauce. Taste curry and add more palm sugar or fish sauce, if needed, to achieve a balance of sweet and salty. Allow curry to cool to room temperature, transfer to an airtight container, and place in the refrigerator to cool completely.

Wearing gloves, cut scallops into quarters on a cool, clean cutting surface. Place scallop meat in a bowl and cover with lime juice. Allow scallops to marinate in lime juice for approximately 4 minutes, stirring once. Add chilled curried corn mixture and sliced onions to the scallop bowl. Mix gently to combine well.

To serve, spoon equal amounts of ceviche into 4 small chilled serving bowls. Garnish with Fried Shallots and lime leaf. Serve immediately.

→ SERVES 4 ←

SCALLOP AND ZHOUG CEVICHE

COCONUT CREAM

HOT SAUCE

LIME

CHOPPY CHOP
PRAWNS

CUCUMBER

CHILI CARAMEL
PORK

COD

CHILI
TAMARIND

ZHENG

PINEAPPLE
TORTILLA

PICKLED SHALLOT

Taco trucks have been a part of North American street-food culture for an extremely long time. They have evolved through the years; alongside traditional Mexican taco trucks and carts, it is now common to see unique and varied flavour combinations from truck to truck. In my opinion, it was Roy Choi from Kogi BBQ in Los Angeles with his Korean tacos and fusion menu that put taco trucks and gourmet food trucks on the map in 2008. This was the real starting point for where the industry is today.

Tacos have been a staple menu item on our truck since day one, and were the impetus to open the truck in the first place. We use tortillas as a serving vessel for globally inspired flavour combinations. The corn tortillas are a means of delivering the food to the mouth. With all of the different types of tacos we have served, there have been several that are the most popular amongst our customers. If we take them off the menu for a time, we have hoards of people pleading with us to bring them back on. One of these, the Crispy Cod Taco with Smoked Pineapple and Habanero Hot Sauce (page 181), is by far the most popular of all. This taco also won the Best Menu Item Award at the inaugural AwesTRUCK Food Truck Awards in 2012.

Another fan favourite, the Hangover Taco, gets an injection here from my cooking days at MECCA Restaurant in Melbourne. There were a couple of Afghani guys in the kitchen at MECCA—Mia, a former tank driver turned dish-pit master and kitchen hand, and Hakim, who would help out anywhere he was needed, always with a smile on his face. Mia and Hakim were both great guys, always good for a morale boost and a solid razzing. The kitchen would be working away, and one of the boys would cook us what they called Afghani eggs. They would grab a whole lot of chili and garlic and throw it in a hot pan with fresh eggs. When the egg whites began to crisp up at the edges, they would break the eggs up slightly, throw in the parsley and cilantro, and give it a good squeeze of lemon juice. The eggs would be served straight from the pan, with warm Turkish bread. Mia would make warm Honey Cardamom Pistachio Milk (page 219) to wash it all down, and we'd all tuck in while we kept working away. Here, I've made these eggs the centre of the Hangover Taco, and trust me, they do the trick.

I love tacos for the ease of serving; they're fun to eat, not too filling, and the options for what you can serve in a tortilla are endless. They are perfect for a snack, or for throwing out family-style amongst a big group of friends. The taco recipes I've included here are designed

TACOS

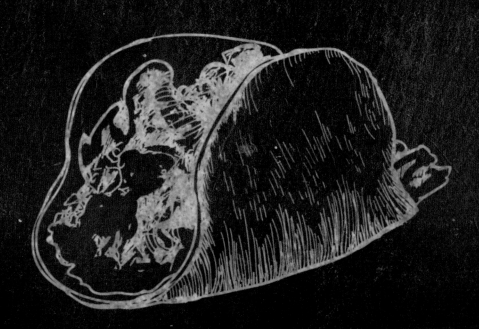

CRISPY COD TACO WITH PICKLED GINGER AND TOBIKO MAYONNAISE

2.2 lb (1 kg) boneless, skinless cod
¼ cup (60 mL) Pickled Ginger (page 241)
1 tsp (5 mL) sesame oil
1 Tbsp (15 mL) light soy sauce
1 tsp (5 mL) mirin
1 cup (250 mL) Mayonnaise (page 266)
2 Tbsp (30 mL) *tobiko*
4 cups (1 L) canola oil
2 cups (500 mL) self-rising flour
1 cup (250 mL) soda water (approx.)
1 cup (250 mL) all-purpose flour
½ English cucumber, peeled, seeded, and
 finely julienned
¼ cup (60 mL) Furikake (page 251)
24 Corn Tortillas (page 252)

Cut the cod into strips the size of a small finger. Set aside in the refrigerator.

In a blender, combine pickled ginger, sesame oil, soy sauce, and mirin. Purée until smooth. Transfer into a small bowl, add Mayonnaise and *tobiko*. Stir to combine well. Transfer to a sauce dish, and place in the refrigerator.

In a large, heavy-bottomed pot, heat canola oil to 350°F (180°C).

Place self-rising flour in a small bowl. Create a well in the centre of the flour; while whisking, slowly add soda water until batter is thin and smooth, similar to the consistency of crepe batter.

Place all-purpose flour into a separate small bowl for dredging.

Dredge cod pieces in all-purpose flour, shake off excess flour, and transfer to batter. One at a time, carefully lift a piece of fish from the batter, shake off excess batter, and carefully place in the oil. Fry cod in small batches for 2 minutes or until golden brown. Remove cod from pot and place on paper towel to absorb excess oil. Repeat this process until all cod is cooked.

Serve cod immediately, family-style, with cucumber, ginger, and *tobiko* mayonnaise, Furikake, and Corn Tortillas.

→» SERVES 4 «←

CHILI CARAMEL PORK BELLY TACO

8 cups (2 L) Master Stock (page 263)
2.2 lb (1 kg) pork belly, skin removed
4 cups (1 L) canola oil
½ cup (125 mL) Chili Caramel (page 265)
1 cup (250 mL) cilantro, leaves picked
1 small red onion, finely diced
24 Corn Tortillas (page 252)
½ English cucumber, julienned
½ cup (125 mL) Chili Tamarind (page 268)
2 limes, cut into wedges

In a large pot, bring Master Stock to a boil over high heat. Once boiling, carefully place pork belly into the stock. Bring stock back to a boil, then reduce heat to medium. Simmer for 1 hour or until pork is tender.

Once cooked, carefully remove the pork belly from the Master Stock. Place pork belly on a tray and allow to cool to room temperature, and then refrigerate until completely chilled.

Once chilled, use a sharp knife to slice pork into pieces ¼ inch (6 mm) thick and 1.5 inches (4 cm) long.

In a large, heavy-bottomed pot, heat oil to 350°F (180°C).

Deep-fry pieces of pork belly for 3 minutes or until pork fat is slightly rendered and turning golden brown. Carefully remove fried pork from pot, allowing excess oil to drain off. Place on paper towel to absorb excess oil.

Place pork belly in a small bowl, and add Chili Caramel. Toss to coat.

In a separate small bowl, combine cilantro and onion.

Serve pork, family-style, with Corn Tortillas, cucumber, Chili Tamarind, onion-cilantro mixture, and lime wedges.

→→ SERVES 4 ←←

CRISPY COD TACO WITH SMOKED PINEAPPLE AND HABANERO HOT SAUCE

2.2 lb (1 kg) boneless, skinless cod

2 cups (500 mL) red cabbage,
  finely shaved

¼ cup (60 mL) white vinegar

1 tsp (5 mL) kosher salt

2 Tbsp (30 mL) superfine sugar

½ cup (125 mL) sour cream

¼ cup (60 mL) fine unsweetened
  shredded coconut, toasted

2 Tbsp (30 mL) Chili Caramel (page 265)

4 cups (1 L) canola oil

2 cups (500 mL) self-rising flour

1 cup (250 mL) soda water (approx.)

1 cup (250 mL) all-purpose flour

1 cup (250 mL) Smoked Pineapple and
  Habanero Hot Sauce (page 269)

24 Corn Tortillas (page 252)

½ cup (125 mL) cilantro leaves,
  roughly chopped

2 limes, cut into wedges

Using a sharp knife, cut cod into strips the size of a small finger. Set aside in the refrigerator.

In a small bowl, combine cabbage, vinegar, salt, and sugar. Mix well. Mix the cabbage occasionally while you are preparing the rest of the dish. Once the cabbage is softened (approximately 10 minutes), transfer cabbage to a serving vessel, shaking off excess pickling liquid. Set aside in the refrigerator.

In a small bowl, combine sour cream, coconut, and Chili Caramel. Mix well, and set aside in the refrigerator.

In a large, heavy-bottomed pot, heat oil to 350°F (180°C).

Place self-rising flour into a small bowl. Create a well in the centre of the flour; while whisking, slowly add soda water until batter reaches a smooth, thin consistency, similar to that of crepe batter.

Place all-purpose flour in a separate small bowl for dredging.

Dredge cod pieces in all-purpose flour, shake off excess flour, and transfer to batter. One at a time, carefully lift a piece of cod from the batter, shake off excess batter, and carefully place in the oil. Deep-fry cod in small batches for 2 minutes or until golden brown. Remove cod from pot and place on paper towel to absorb excess oil. Repeat this process until all cod is cooked.

Serve cod immediately, family-style, with the pickled cabbage, Smoked Pineapple Habanero Hot Sauce, coconut sour cream, Corn Tortillas, cilantro, and lime wedges.

→→ SERVES 4 ←←

CRISPY PORK AND GRILLED PINEAPPLE TACO

2.2 lb (1 kg) boneless pork loin, cut crosswise into ½-inch (1 cm) thick slices

½ cup (125 mL) whole milk

2 large eggs

1 cup (250 mL) all-purpose flour

2 cups (500 mL) panko bread crumbs

1 pineapple, peeled, cored, and quartered

4 cups (1 L) canola oil

1 small red onion, finely diced

1 cup (250 mL) cilantro leaves, finely chopped

24 Corn Tortillas (page 252)

1 cup (250 mL) Smoked Tomato Aioli (page 272)

Lay 2 pork slices between 2 pieces of plastic wrap. Using a mallet, gently tenderize the pork by evenly pounding the surface. Repeat this process until all pork slices have been tenderized.

Preheat barbecue or indoor grill to highest setting.

In a small bowl, combine milk and eggs. Set aside at room temperature.

Set up a dredging station, with flour, milk-egg mixture, and panko each in separate bowls, in that order.

Place pineapple on the barbecue, and grill for 4 minutes or until it has caramelized on each side. Remove from grill, and allow to cool slightly at room temperature. Once cooled, use a sharp knife to cut pineapple into bite-sized pieces; place in a bowl, and set aside at room temperature.

Working in batches, dredge pork slices in flour, then soak in egg-milk mixture. Transfer to panko, and set aside on a tray in the refrigerator until ready to cook.

In a large, heavy-bottomed pot, heat oil to 350°F (180°C).

Working with 1 or 2 slices of pork at a time, deep-fry pork in oil for 2 to 3 minutes or until golden brown. Remove cooked pork from pot, and place on paper towel to absorb excess oil. Repeat this process until all pork slices are cooked.

Combine red onion and cilantro. Mix well, and place in a small serving bowl.

Cut the pork slices into strips. Serve tacos family-style, with Corn Tortillas, pork, pineapple, cilantro-onion mixture, and Smoked Tomato Aioli.

» SERVES 4 «

CRISPY PRAWN TACO WITH PICKLED SHALLOTS AND ZHOUG

4 cups (1 L) canola oil

2 cups (500 mL) self-rising flour

1 cup (250 mL) soda water (approx.)

1 cup (250 mL) all-purpose flour

24 extra large tiger prawns, shelled, deveined, and heads and tails removed

1 cup (250 mL) Pickled Shallots (page 243)

½ cup (125 mL) Zhoug (page 274)

½ English cucumber, peeled and seeded, finely julienned

24 Corn Tortillas (page 252)

½ cup (125 mL) cilantro leaves, roughly chopped

2 limes, cut into wedges

In a large, heavy-bottomed pot, heat oil to 350°F (180°C).

Place self-rising flour in a small bowl. Create a well in the centre of the flour; while whisking, slowly add soda water until batter reaches a smooth, thin consistency, similar to crepe batter.

Place all-purpose flour in a separate small bowl for dredging.

Dredge prawns in all-purpose flour, shake off excess flour, and transfer to batter. One at a time, carefully lift prawns from the batter, shake off excess batter, and carefully place into the hot oil. Deep-fry prawns in small batches for 3 to 4 minutes or until golden brown. Remove prawns from pot and place on paper towel to absorb excess oil. Repeat this process until all prawns are cooked.

Serve prawns immediately, family-style, with Pickled Shallots, Zhoug, cucumber, Corn Tortillas, cilantro, and lime wedges.

→→ SERVES 4 ←←

DESSERTS

I have always loved dessert. My favourite dessert in the world is soufflé. The potential flavour combinations of this soft, airy cake are endless. Unfortunately, achieving a soufflé in a truck would be impossible, what with the time it takes to prepare and cook the soufflé from the moment it is ordered. If anyone can pull off a soufflé truck and make it work, I will be in line every day!

We don't often serve desserts from the truck, but when we do, they're made for easy and fast service. That being said, for whatever reason, I seem to forget that notion whenever I put the fried bananas on the menu and have to juggle the other dishes that use the same small deep-fryer. This dessert has proved to be a hugely popular dish, though, and like the crispy cod taco, it is requested on a regular basis.

The following recipes are simple and use a lot of fresh seasonal fruit, all of which can be served individually or family-style. A selection can be made and spread across a large table of people to pass around. The vibrant colours and flavours will be an attractive feast in any situation.

DESSERTS

BEATRIX LAMINGTONS **197**

COCONUT STICKY RICE WITH MANGO AND TOASTED
COCONUT CREAM **201**

COCONUT TAPIOCA AND PINEAPPLE PUDDING **202**

ETON MESS **203**

FRESH AND PICKLED WATERMELON AND FRIED BANANA
WITH TOASTED COCONUT CREAM **204**

FRESH FRUIT AND SWEET CHILI FISH SALTS **206**

GRILLED LIME AND JALAPEÑO SORBET **207**

SUMMER PUDDING **208**

TOASTED COCONUT CONDENSED MILK ICE CREAM **209**

GRANITAS

GINGER WINE AND MANGO GRANITA **211**

HONEYDEW MELON AND ICE WINE GRANITA **212**

SMOKED PINEAPPLE AND BOURBON GRANITA **213**

WATERMELON, GIN, AND THAI BASIL GRANITA **214**

BEATRIX LAMINGTONS

RECIPE BY GUEST CHEF: NAT PAULL, BEATRIX BAKERY, MELBOURNE

1 cup (250 mL) Strawberry Jam (page 199)

1 cup (250 mL) + 4 tsp (20 mL) superfine sugar, divided

1 Tbsp (15 mL) canola oil (approx)

1⅔ cups (400 mL) egg (approx. 7 large eggs)

½ cup (125 mL) + 2 Tbsp (30 mL) + 3½ Tbsp (50 mL) unsalted butter

1 tsp (5 mL) vanilla extract

1 cup (250 mL) + 4 tsp (20 mL) all-purpose flour

1 tsp (5 mL) fine salt

2 cups (500 mL) unsweetened shredded coconut

2 cups (500 mL) icing sugar

3½ Tbsp (50 mL) good-quality Dutch or baking cocoa

2 Tbsp (30 mL) water

½ cup (125 mL) + 2 Tbsp (30 mL) heavy cream

> When preparing the sponge cake, a precise measurement of egg is very important. Crack the eggs into a small bowl, one at a time, and add the eggs to a measuring cup individually until you reach 1⅔ cups (410 mL) of eggs. If you need to lightly whisk a partial egg to reach the desired amount before adding it to the measuring cup, you can do so, but be careful not to over whisk the egg.

Nat Paull is the chef and owner of Beatrix Bakery in North Melbourne. I met Nat when I started at MECCA for the second half of my apprenticeship. Nat is a magician in the kitchen, a true talent with an eye for perfection. We gelled straight away, and she took me under her wing. Nat and I always had a playful, joking connection, creating characters and running jokes for the entire kitchen. One of the characters I came up with, a German chef called Gerhard Schtickentappen, was a favourite of Nat's and the entire staff at MECCA. On my last day at MECCA, Nat had T-shirts made that said on the front, "Who is Gerhard Schtickentappen?", with a picture of me in character. The entire staff of MECCA was wearing this T-shirt. Nat's relaxed and playful demeanour, while being dead serious when needed, is the perfect personality for inspiring a creative feel in the kitchen.

Prepare Strawberry Jam at least 1 day in advance, 3 days is ideal.

On the day of use, simmer jam for 15 minutes over low heat.

 Nat suggests an extra simmer on the third day and refrigerating overnight to make it a little thicker.

On the serving day, prepare the sponge cake, cocoa icing, and toasted coconut. To prepare the sponge cake, line a 10-inch (25 cm) square pan with parchment paper, using canola oil to stick the sides down, but don't oil the top of the paper.

Preheat oven to 335°C (170°F).

Build a double boiler by placing a heat-proof bowl over a pot of barely simmering water, making sure that the bottom of the bowl does not touch the water. Place sugar and all of the eggs in the bowl, and heat, gently stirring to prevent catching, for 2 to 3 minutes or until hot to the touch.

Pop the mixer bowl onto a stand mixer or use an electric hand mixer to whisk the egg mixture on medium-high speed for 8 minutes or until pale, fluffy, and can hold a peak.

While whisking, heat ½ cup (125 mL) plus 2 Tbsp (30 mL) of butter in a saucepan over low heat for 5 minutes or until the butter starts to turn a toasty brown. Remove from heat, and add vanilla. Mix to combine, and set aside at room temperature.

In a small bowl, combine 1 cup (250 mL) of flour and salt. Mix to combine, and set aside at room temperature.

Continued on next page

COCONUT STICKY RICE WITH MANGO AND TOASTED COCONUT CREAM

2 cups (500 mL) glutinous rice

1 cup (250 mL) coconut milk

¼ cup (60 mL) palm sugar, shaved

2 mangoes, peeled and cut into ⅛-inch (3 mm) thick slices

½ cup (125 mL) Toasted Coconut Cream (page 273)

4 kaffir lime leaves, spines removed and finely julienned

> You must use glutinous rice to achieve the desired stickiness in the coconut rice. You can find glutinous rice at most Asian grocers and some specialty food retailers.

This is a classic Thai dessert, served at restaurants and street stalls. It would be an unexpected finale for your dinner party, and can be eaten for a quick breakfast the next day.

Place rice into a resealable container and cover completely with cold water. Cover and place in the refrigerator and for a minimum of 6 hours to soak.

In a small pot, gently warm coconut milk and palm sugar over medium-low heat until sugar has dissolved. Remove from heat, and set aside at room temperature.

Set up a steamer over boiling water. Cut a sheet of cheesecloth large enough to overhang the steamer basket. Soak the cheesecloth in cold water and squeeze dry. Lay cheesecloth in the steamer basket.

Strain the rice through a strainer, and rinse under cold running water until water runs clear. Place rice in the steamer in a thin, even layer. Fold the excess cheesecloth over the rice and place the lid on the steamer basket. Steam for 20 minutes or until rice is cooked through and sticky.

Remove rice from the steamer and place in a bowl. Add coconut milk-mixture. Stir to combine, and set aside at room temperature.

To serve, place equal spoonfuls of sticky rice on each serving plate. Lay the sliced mango fanned out across the top of the rice. Dress with Toasted Coconut Cream, and garnish with lime leaves. Serve immediately.

→ SERVES 4 ←

FRIED BANANA WITH TOASTED COCONUT CREAM

4 cups (1 L) canola oil

1½ cups (375 mL) self-rising flour
(approx.), divided

1 cup (250 mL) soda water

2 bananas, halved lengthwise

¼ cup (60 mL) Toasted Coconut Cream
(page 273)

2 kaffir lime leaves, spines removed and
finely julienned

4 sprigs mint, leaves picked

This dessert is the ideal food-truck treat. It is quick and simple to prepare, and a crowd favourite. The bananas come out of the deep-fryer golden and crispy on the outside, and warm and almost gooey on the inside.

In a deep-fryer or deep pot, heat oil to 350°F (180°C).

Place 1 cup (250 mL) of flour in a medium mixing bowl. Gradually add soda water to flour, whisking until batter is smooth but not too runny, similar to pancake batter.

Dredge banana pieces in ½ cup (125 mL) of flour, and then in batter. Carefully place battered banana pieces in hot oil and deep-fry for 3 minutes or until golden brown. Remove pieces from pot and place on paper towel to absorb excess oil.

To serve, place one banana piece on each serving plate, flattest side down. Using a teaspoon, place dots of Toasted Coconut Cream on each fritter and on each plate. Sprinkle with lime leaves and garnish with mint leaves. Serve immediately.

» SERVES 4 «

GRANITAS

Granitas are semi-frozen desserts made from water, sugar, and flavouring ingredients like fresh fruit. The freezing and forking technique creates a coarse, crystalline texture. The granita recipes here can be used in multiple ways. I like to eat them on their own or use them as garnishes for desserts or cocktails. Get inventive and experiment with their refreshing uses for yourself.

GINGER WINE AND MANGO GRANITA

4 ripe mangoes, peeled and pitted
1 cup (250 mL) water
2 cups (500 mL) ginger wine
superfine sugar, to taste

Ginger wine is made from ground ginger root and raisins. It was first produced in England, but is now popular worldwide.

In a blender, purée mango with water until smooth. Transfer puréed mango mixture to a bowl, and add ginger wine and sugar to desired sweetness. Mix well. Place mixture into a large, shallow glass casserole dish, and place in the freezer. Allow mixture to freeze completely.

Once frozen, scrape the surface of the frozen mixture with a fork to break it up into icy granules. At this point, it is ready to serve as desired. Store the remaining granita mixture in the freezer, covered tightly with plastic wrap.

↠ MAKES 4 CUPS (1 L) ↞

WATERMELON, GIN, AND THAI BASIL GRANITA

1 small seedless watermelon, roughly cubed

1 cup (250 mL) Thai basil leaves

1 cup (250 mL) gin

superfine sugar, to taste

I recommend using Dillon's Small Batch Distiller's Unfiltered Gin 22 for this recipe (available online), as the botanicals in the gin complement the fresh Thai basil and sweet watermelon in the granita without overpowering it with a strong juniper flavour common to some other gins.

In a blender, purée watermelon and basil until smooth. Transfer to a bowl and combine with gin. Add sugar to desired sweetness. Mix well. Place mixture into a large, shallow, glass casserole dish, and place in the freezer. Allow mixture to freeze completely.

To serve, scrape the surface of the frozen mixture with a fork. Serve in a glass on its own, or use as a garnish for cocktails or other desserts. Store the remaining granita mixture in the freezer, covered tightly with plastic wrap.

→ MAKES 6 CUPS (1.5 L) ←

DRINKS

We don't serve the typical bottled or canned beverages from our truck. Instead, we opt to make our own drinks, often showcasing seasonal fruits and herbs. Fruited iced teas and lemonades are frequently on the menu during the warmer months. The following drink recipes include some that have been featured on the truck, and others that will pair perfectly with any of the recipes found in this book. They are refreshing and satisfying enough to enjoy on their own, as well. Serve them at your next dinner party or barbeque. Have a selection of pitchers on the table for everyone to share. Don't be afraid to add a little booze to them, if desired.

DRINKS

CHILI AND MINT LIMEADE

1 cup (250 mL) mint leaves

10 limes, quartered

4 bird's eye chilies, seeded

1 Tbsp (15 mL) kosher salt

8 cups (2 L) cold water

superfine sugar, to taste

In a large pitcher, muddle mint, limes, chilies, and salt. Pour cold water into pitcher and add sugar to desired sweetness. Stir to combine and refrigerate for a minimum of 2 hours.

Serve in a glass over ice.

→ MAKES 9 CUPS (2.25 L) ←

CUCUMBER AND MINT LASSI

2 cups (500 mL) full-fat plain Greek yogurt

1 cup (250 mL) sparkling water

1 cup (250 mL) mint leaves

1 English cucumber, peeled and seeded, cubed

1 tsp (5 mL) kosher salt

1 cup (250 mL) ice cubes

1 Tbsp (15 mL) dried mint

In a large pitcher, combine yogurt, sparkling water, mint leaves, cucumber, salt, and ice.

Using an immersion blender, purée until smooth and frothy. Pass mixture through a fine sieve into a clean pitcher.

Serve chilled in glasses, dusted with dried mint.

→ MAKES 6 CUPS (1.5 L) ←

HONEY, CARDAMOM, AND PISTACHIO MILK

4 cups (1 L) whole milk

6 cardamom pods, cracked

¼ cup (60 mL) unsalted pistachios, finely chopped

honey, to taste

This drink was introduced to me by Hakim, an Afghani kitchen hand/ prep chef I worked with while I was apprenticing at MECCA restaurant in Melbourne. Hakim was a much loved member of the team. He used to make breakfast for the kitchen staff, and would serve this drink alongside what he called Afghani Eggs (page 187). It is the perfect start to a long work day.

In a pot, bring milk, cardamom, and pistachios to a simmer over medium-high heat. Turn off heat, and add honey to desired sweetness.

Serve warm in a tall glass.

→ MAKES 4 CUPS (1 L) ←

MOROCCAN MINT TEA

¼ cup (60 mL) gunpowder tea leaves
1 cup (250 mL) mint leaves, divided
4 cups water
superfine sugar, to taste

> It is best to use a large, Middle Eastern tea pot for serving.
>
> Gunpowder tea leaves can be found at most specialty tea shops, and are widely available at Middle Eastern and Asian grocers.

One of my favourite drinks is Moroccan Mint Tea. Served throughout the Middle East, mint tea is the perfect beverage for putting a smile on your face. On my travels through Morocco, mint tea was served at cafes, restaurants, and on the street and by friendly shopkeepers while trying to barter for your business.

In a large Middle Eastern teapot, place tea leaves and three-quarters of the mint.

In a medium pot, bring water to a boil over high heat. Carefully pour boiling water into the teapot, and steep for approximately 5 minutes before stretching the tea.

To stretch the tea, gently trickle the tea from the teapot into a Moroccan tea glass, gradually increasing the distance between the teapot and the glass. Pour the contents of the glass back into the teapot, and repeat this process a minimum of 10 times.

Pick leaves from remaining mint, and divide equally across tea glasses. Sweeten the tea in the teapot with sugar, if desired. Pour tea into tea glasses. Serve immediately.

⇒ MAKES 4 CUPS (1 L) ⇐

TOM YUM CAESAR

¼ cup (60 mL) Sweet Chili Fish Salt, for rimming (page 206)

8 large ice cubes

4 oz (120 mL) Dillon's Small Batch Distillers' Method 95 Vodka, or similar quality vodka

4 cups (1 L) Chilled Clam Tom Yum Soup Broth (page 57)

Angelica bitters, to taste

Worcestershire sauce, to taste

2 Tbsp (30 mL) Chili Jam (page 266)

juice of 2 limes

¼ cup (60 mL) Fried Shallots (page 250)

4 stalks lemongrass, bruised with the back of the blade of a knife

Angelica bitters have a strong celery-like flavour, derived from the Angelica plant.

I recommend using Dillon's Small Batch Distillers' Angelica bitters, available online.

The Tom Yum Caesar was concocted in collaboration with our friends at Dillon's Small Batch Distillers. It is a great take on a Canadian classic; the chilled Tom Yum broth adds a complex flavour profile, and is the perfect kick-start to the day when served with breakfast and a friendly amount of vodka.

Rim glasses with Sweet Chili Fish Salt. Add 2 ice cubes to each glass. Pour 1 oz (28 mL) of vodka and 1 cup (250 mL) of Chilled Tom Yum Soup Broth into each glass. Top off with desired amounts of Angelica bitters, Worcestershire sauce, Chili Jam, and lime juice. Garnish with Fried Shallots and serve immediately with lemongrass swizzle sticks.

→ MAKES 5 CUPS (1.25 L) ←

WATERMELON AND THAI BASIL LEMONADE

½ seedless watermelon, cubed

3 cups (750 mL) Thai basil leaves

3 lemons, quartered

1 tsp (5 mL) kosher salt

4 cups (1 L) cold water

superfine sugar, to taste

In a large pitcher, muddle watermelon, basil, lemons, and salt. Pour water into pitcher, and add sugar to desired sweetness. Place in the refrigerator to steep for a minimum of 2 hours.

Serve in a glass over ice.

→ MAKES 8 CUPS (2 L) ←

The recipes in this section are for stocking your larder. These can be made well in advance and stored until they are needed. A lot of these recipes have been picked up and adapted throughout my career from all of the chefs I have worked for.

I make a point of making everything from scratch for the truck. I take pride in the fact that every sauce or condiment or garnish that is served from the truck window has been made by me.

It's not hard to start building your larder. When you have a free day, get the kids together and make some stuff. Store it properly, and it's there for when you need it. A well-stocked larder is an inspiring thing to look at; everything neatly labelled and stored. The selection of items can get the creative juices flowing. It will also make most of the recipes in this book way less daunting due to the fact that most items are sitting a finger's reach away from you.

HARISSA

4 medium red bell peppers
1 tsp (5 mL) cumin seeds
2 Tbsp (30 mL) coriander seeds
6 cloves garlic
20 red long Thai chilies, seeded
20 red long Thai chilies (whole)
½ cup (125 mL) grape seed oil
kosher salt, to taste

Harissa is a Tunisian chili paste, but is common throughout the Middle East and North Africa. The following recipe is inspired by what I remember of the recipe we used at MECCA in Melbourne, working under Cath Claringbold.

Holding the red peppers with heatproof tongs over a naked flame, blister the peppers until skin is completely blackened. Alternatively, you can blacken the peppers on a barbeque or grill set to its highest heat setting, rotating the peppers until the skin is evenly blackened. Place blistered peppers in a bowl and cover bowl tightly with plastic wrap. Set aside and allow peppers to steam while cooling. When peppers have cooled, discard skin and seeds and set peppers aside at room temperature.

In a dry pan, toast cumin and coriander seeds, tossing continually, for 3 minutes over high heat or until aromatic. Remove seeds from pan and set aside at room temperature to cool.

In a clean spice grinder, finely grind cooled toasted cumin and coriander seeds.

 Do not grind while hot as spice will burn.

In a food processor, combine garlic, chilies, and ground spices. Process until smooth. Add roasted peppers and pulse until smooth.

 Over-puréeing the mixture will turn its colour to orange rather than a desired deep red.

Transfer mixture to a bowl, and add 115 mL of grape seed oil. Gently stir to combine. Season with salt, and transfer to an airtight container. Seal the surface of the harissa with 2 tsp (10 mL) of grape seed oil and cover with a lid. Store in the refrigerator for up to 2 weeks.

→ MAKES 2¼ CUPS (560 ML) ←

CUMIN SALT

CUMIN SALT

½ cup (125 mL) kosher salt
½ cup (125 mL) cumin seeds

In a food processor, pulse salt until fine. Transfer ground salt into a bowl.

In a dry pan, lightly toast cumin seeds over high heat for 2 minutes or until aromatic. Remove seeds from pan and set aside at room temperature until cool.

In a clean spice grinder, finely grind cooled cumin seeds. Remove from grinder and combine with ground salt.

Transfer to an airtight container and store at room temperature for up to 3 months.

→ MAKES 1 CUP (250 ML) ←

FIVE SPICE

6 cardamom pods, cracked and
 seeds removed
5 whole star anise
2 sticks cinnamon, broken
3 Tbsp (45 mL) Szechuan peppercorns
3 Tbsp (45 mL) kosher salt
2 tsp (10 mL) ground nutmeg

Five Spice is an earthy, peppery, and aromatic blend of spices that is integral to a lot of Chinese cooking. The spices in this blend, particularly star anise, help to bring out the flavours of proteins like pork and beef.

In a dry pan, dry-roast cardamom, star anise, cinnamon, Szechuan peppercorns, and salt over medium heat for 2 to 3 minutes or until fragrant. Stir constantly to avoid burning. Remove pan from heat and transfer spices to a bowl. Allow spices to cool completely.

Using a mortar and pestle or clean spice grinder, grind the mixture to a fine powder, and add nutmeg.

Transfer to an airtight container and store at room temperature for up to 3 months.

→ MAKES 9 TBSP (135 ML) ←

DRY AND WET CHERMOULA

DRY CHERMOULA

1 Tbsp (15 mL) ground coriander seeds

1½ tsp (7 mL) sweet paprika

1 tsp (5 mL) ground ginger

1 tsp (5 mL) ground cumin

½ tsp (2 mL) freshly ground black pepper

½ tsp (2 mL) chili powder

½ tsp (2 mL) garlic powder

1 tsp (5 mL) icing sugar

kosher salt, to taste

WET CHERMOULA

½ cup (125 mL) flaked almonds

½ cup (125 mL) flat leaf parsley leaves

½ cup (125 mL) cilantro leaves

3 bird's eye chilies, seeded

1 batch Dry Chermoula (page 234)

3 cloves garlic, minced

juice of 1 lemon

½ cup (125 mL) olive oil

kosher salt, to taste

Chermoula is used heavily in Morocco and Tunisia, where recipes will differ from town to town. Chermoula can be either a dry spice blend (Dry Chermoula) or a wet paste (Wet Chermoula) used for seasoning or marinating fish or meat. One of my favourite uses of Dry Chermoula is to season prawns, like in the Chermoula Prawn and Marinated Pepper Salad recipe (page 149). I love using Wet Chermoula for marinating meats, but after some playing around, I discovered it is also a unique way to flavour tartare, like in the Lamb Tartare with Chermoula recipe (page 94).

DRY CHERMOULA

In a small bowl, combine all spices and icing sugar. Season to taste with salt.

Transfer to an airtight container and store at room temperature for up to 3 months.

➤ MAKES 5 TBSP (75 ML) ◄

WET CHERMOULA

In a dry pan, toast almonds for approximately 5 minutes over high heat, tossing continually. Remove from pan and set aside to cool. Once cooled, crush in mortar and pestle until coarse. Set aside at room temperature.

Finely chop parsley, cilantro, and bird's eye chilies.

In a bowl, combine Dry Chermoula, garlic, chilies, herbs, lemon juice, olive oil, and crushed almond flakes. Mix well, and season to taste with salt, if necessary.

Transfer to an airtight container and store in the refrigerator for up to 1 month.

➤ MAKES 2 CUPS (500 ML) ◄

WET CHERMOULA

DUKKAH

KOFTA SPICE

2 Tbsp (30 mL) ground allspice
2 Tbsp (30 mL) paprika
3 Tbsp (45 mL) dried mint
1 Tbsp (15 mL) Za'atar (page 238)
1 tsp (5 mL) ground cinnamon
1 tsp (5 mL) ground coriander

This is a spice blend used for flavouring *kofta*, which is a ground lamb meatball common in the Middle East and North Africa.

In a small bowl, combine all ingredients and mix well.

Transfer to an airtight container and store at room temperature for up to 3 months.

→ MAKES 9 TBSP (135 ML) ←

DUKKAH

1 cup (250 mL) sesame seeds, toasted
½ cup (125 mL) hazelnuts, roasted and
  rubbed to remove skin
¼ cup (60 mL) cumin seeds, toasted
¼ cup (60 mL) coriander seeds, toasted
kosher salt, to taste

Dukkah is a nutty and aromatic Egyptian seasoning blend, best served with fresh Turkish bread and olive oil for dipping. It is also great when used for seasoning fish and lamb, or putting in sauces and salads.

Using a mortar and pestle, lightly crush sesame seeds until fragrant. Separately, crush hazelnuts and remaining spices until fine.

In a bowl, add crushed ingredients and combine thoroughly. Season with salt.

Transfer to an airtight container and store at room temperature for up to 2 weeks.

→ MAKES 2 CUPS (500 ML) ←

> To toast spices, preheat oven to 350° F (180° C). Place seeds in a tray or small pan and toast in oven, tossing occasionally, until aromatic and golden brown, 5–10 minutes.

ZA'ATAR

1 cup (250 mL) *za'atar*
¼ cup (60 mL) sumac
¼ cup (60 mL) sesame seeds, toasted

Za'atar is available at Middle Eastern grocery stores.

Za'atar is an Arabic word that is used to refer to a family of herbs including oregano and thyme, but also refers to a blend of dried *za'atar*, sesame seeds, and sumac. This blend is used heavily in the Middle East for seasoning meats, fish, flatbreads, salads, and more. It is extremely aromatic, and with the addition of sumac, has a citrusy tang.

In a bowl, combine all ingredients, and mix well.

Transfer to an airtight container and store at room temperature for up to 3 months.

→ MAKES 1½ CUPS (375 ML) ←

RAS EL HANOUT

2 Tbsp (30 mL) coriander seeds
1 Tbsp (15 mL) cumin seeds
1 Tbsp (15 mL) fennel seeds
1 Tbsp (15 mL) caraway seeds
1 Tbsp (15 mL) paprika
1 tsp (5 mL) ground cayenne pepper
1 tsp (5 mL) ground turmeric
1 Tbsp (15 mL) ground cinnamon
½ tsp (2 mL) ground cardamom
½ tsp (2 mL) ground nutmeg
1 tsp (5 mL) freshly cracked black pepper
1 Tbsp (15 mL) ground allspice
1 Tbsp (15 mL) ground star anise
kosher salt, to taste

Ras el hanout translates to "head of the shop", and refers to a shop-keeper or chef's signature blend of spices. Every shop and household has its own specific blend. Blends can range from 12 to well over 30 spices. My blend has evolved from Cath Claringbold's recipe at MECCA, which is where I was first exposed to it. *Ras el hanout* is a bold spice blend that can be used for spicing tagines and soups or rubbing meats and fish, and is used in many sauces and dressings.

In a dry pan, toast coriander, cumin, fennel, and caraway seeds, tossing continually, for 3 minutes over high heat or until aromatic. Remove seeds from pan and set aside at room temperature to cool.

In a clean spice grinder, finely grind cooled toasted seeds.

 Do not grind while hot as spices will burn.

In a small bowl, combine all ingredients, and mix well.

Transfer to an airtight container and store at room temperature for up to 3 months.

→ MAKES 10 TBSP (150 ML) ←

ZA'ATAR

PICKLED FENNEL

4–6 fennel bulbs

4 red shallots

½ cup (125 mL) dill fronds

1 lemon (peel only)

¼ cup (60 mL) tarragon leaves

4 cloves garlic, sliced

6 cups (1.5 L) water

1¼ cups (310 mL) white vinegar

3 Tbsp (45 mL) white sugar

3 Tbsp (45 mL) kosher salt

1 tsp (5 mL) whole black peppercorns

2 Tbsp (30 mL) coriander seeds

You will need two 4-cup (1 L) sterilized canning jars.

Pickling fennel, which has an inherent anise or licorice flavour, helps to bring out the flavour of meats like beef and pork. Pickled fennel also adds a beautiful crunch and freshness when mixed through a herb salad.

Sterilize canning jars (see method on page 240).

Using a sharp knife, remove the base and woody sprigs from the fennel bulbs. Place fennel base side up on a cutting board. Cut fennel in half, through the centre of the bulb. Following the grain, cut fennel lengthwise into ½-inch (1 cm) wedges. Place in a bowl, and set aside at room temperature.

Using a mandolin or sharp knife, slice shallots into rings, approximately ⅛ inch (3 mm) thick. Place in a bowl, and set aside at room temperature.

In the canning jars, stack fennel wedges, dill, lemon peel, tarragon, shallots, and garlic slices in layers until jars are completely filled.

Fill a large pot with the water. Add vinegar, sugar, salt, peppercorns, and coriander seeds. Bring to a boil over high heat. Turn off heat.

Carefully pour hot pickling liquid over the contents in the jars until the liquid reaches the rims. Carefully agitate the jars to release any pockets of air captured inside. Seal jars with lids, and set aside to cool at room temperature. Use your finger to check that jars are sealed. The lid should not spring back when pressed, but remain firmly in place.

Once cooled, unopened jars can be stored in a cool, dry place for up to 1 year and opened jars can be stored in the refrigerator for up to 1 month.

→ MAKES 8 CUPS (2 L) ←

PICKLED WATERMELON

1 small seedless watermelon

4 red shallots

½ cup (125 mL) tarragon leaves

6 cups (1.5 L) water

1¼ cups (310 mL) white vinegar

3 Tbsp (45 mL) white sugar

3 Tbsp (45 mL) kosher salt

1 tsp (5 mL) whole black peppercorns

2 Tbsp (30 mL) coriander seeds

> You will need two 4-cup (1 L) sterilized canning jars.

Pickling watermelon adds a salty, tangy kick to the fresh sweetness of the fruit. If you're pickling the flesh of a watermelon, or using the flesh in any other way, you might as well pickle the rind as well instead of throwing it in the compost. Pickling the rind preserves it, and pickled watermelon rind can be used in a similar way as any other pickle.

Sterilize canning jars (see method on page 240).

Using a sharp knife, peel watermelon, reserving the rind for another use, if desired. Cut watermelon flesh into ½-inch (1 cm) cubes. Place in a bowl, and set aside at room temperature.

Using a mandolin or sharp knife, slice shallots into rings, approximately ⅛ inch (3 mm) thick. Place in a bowl, and set aside at room temperature.

In the canning jars, stack watermelon cubes, shallots and tarragon in layers until jars are completely filled.

Fill a large pot with the water. Add vinegar, sugar, salt, peppercorns, and coriander seeds. Bring to a boil over high heat. Turn off heat.

Carefully pour hot pickling liquid over the contents in the jars until the liquid reaches the rims. Carefully agitate the jars to release any pockets of air captured inside. Seal jars with lids, and set aside to cool. Use your finger to check that jars are sealed. The lid should not spring back when pressed, but remain firmly in place.

Once cooled, unopened jars can be stored in a cool, dry place for up to 1 year and opened jars can be stored in the refrigerator for up to 1 month.

⇒ MAKES 8 CUPS (2 L) ⇐

PICKLED WATERMELON RIND

1 small seedless watermelon (rind only)

4 red shallots

6 cups (1.5 L) water

1¼ cups (310 mL) white vinegar

3 Tbsp (45 mL) white sugar

3 Tbsp (45 mL) kosher salt

1 tsp (5 mL) whole black peppercorns

2 Tbsp (30 mL) coriander seeds

1 lemon (peel only)

½ cup (125 mL) tarragon leaves

You will need two 4-cup (1 L) sterilized canning jars.

Sterilize canning jars (see method on page 240).

Using a sharp knife, cut watermelon rind into manageable lengths, approximately 2 inches (5 cm) long. Very carefully, remove the white flesh from the green outer skin of the watermelon, discarding the green skin. Place the white rind in a bowl, and set aside at room temperature.

Using a mandolin or sharp knife, slice shallots into rings, approximately ⅛ inch (3 mm) thick. Place in a bowl, and set aside at room temperature.

Fill a large pot with the water. Add vinegar, sugar, salt, peppercorns, and coriander seeds. Bring to a boil over high heat.

Carefully place watermelon rind in pickling liquid, reduce heat to low and simmer for 10 minutes or until tender. Carefully remove watermelon rind from pickling liquid, and set aside at room temperature.

In the canning jars, stack watermelon rind, lemon peel, shallots, and tarragon in layers until jars are completely filled.

Carefully pour hot pickling liquid over the contents in the jars until the liquid reaches the rims. Carefully agitate the jars to release any pockets of air captured inside. Seal jars with lids, and set aside at room temperature to cool. Use your finger to check that jars are sealed. The lid should not spring back when pressed, but remain firmly in place.

Once cooled, unopened jars can be stored in a cool, dry place for up to 1 year and opened jars can be stored in the refrigerator for up to 1 month.

→ MAKES 8 CUPS (2 L) ←

PRESERVED LEMONS

8–12 lemons

1⅔ cups (410 mL) coarse sea salt (approx.)

¼ cup (60 mL) coriander seeds,
  lightly crushed

3 whole star anise

1 cinnamon stick

2¾ cups (685 mL) water

1¼ cups (310 mL) lemon juice

You will need one sterilized
8 cup (2 L) canning jar.

Preserved lemons can be used in diverse ways, from adding an unexpected zest to otherwise heavy risottos to using as a marinade ingredient for meat and seafood. I love to toss finely julienned preserved lemon rinds in salads to add a fresh zing.

Wash and pat dry lemons. Cut lemons into wedges lengthwise, three-quarters of the way down the lemon, keeping one end of the lemon intact and creating a bloom-like effect. Place "blooming" lemons in resealable freezer bags and place in freezer for approximately 24 hours.

Remove lemons from freezer and allow to thaw completely.

Sterilize canning jar (see method page 240).

Working with one lemon at a time, stuff the centre of each lemon with approximately 2 Tbsp (30 mL) of salt and a pinch of coriander seeds. Set aside at room temperature once stuffed.

Working in layers, carefully place stuffed lemons into the jar, sprinkling each layer with additional salt and coriander seeds. When jar is half full, add star anise and cinnamon stick before proceeding with remaining lemons. Fill jar to rim.

In a container or bowl, combine water and lemon juice. Carefully pour lemon water over jar's contents until jar is full to the rim. Carefully agitate the jar to release any pockets of air captured inside, and tightly seal with lid.

Place a canning jar rack at the bottom of a large pot to insulate the jar from the direct heat at the bottom of the pot. If you do not have a canning jar rack, you can place a thick piece of cardboard at the bottom of the pot. It will become soggy in the boiling process, but will help insulate the jar. Place the jar of lemons on the rack and fill the pot with enough water to come halfway up the side of the jar. Bring water to a boil over high heat and boil for 10 minutes. Remove from heat, and allow jar to cool to room temperature in pot. Use your finger to check that the jar is sealed. The lid should not spring back when pressed, but remain firmly in place.

Once jar is cooled, remove jar from pot. Store in a dry, cool place for a minimum of 1 month before opening. Preserved lemons can be stored unopened indefinitely; once opened refrigerated for up to 3 months.

→ MAKES ONE 8-CUP (2 L) JAR ←

CANDIED BACON

2.2 lb (1 kg) single-smoked bacon, very
thinly sliced (approx. 30 slices)
1 cup (250 mL) dark brown
sugar (approx.)
½ cup (125 mL) honey (approx.)

> Ask your local butcher or
> delicatessen to slice the
> single-smoked bacon very
> thinly, approximately ⅟₃₂ inch
> (1 mm) in thickness, or
> between a slice and a shave.

When candying bacon, the quantities of sugar and honey are not strict, and will vary depending on how heavy-handed you are when layering the bacon, sugar, and honey.

In a glass casserole dish or a large flat-bottomed dish, arrange a layer of bacon slices without overlapping. Lightly sprinkle the surface with brown sugar, and then lightly dress the surface with honey. Arrange a second layer of bacon on top of the first, and lightly sprinkle with brown sugar only. Arrange a third layer of bacon on top, and lightly sprinkle with brown sugar and honey. Repeat this process until all bacon has been layered, alternating between sugar-only and sugar-and-honey layers. Cover layered bacon with plastic wrap and refrigerate overnight.

Preheat oven to 350°F (180°C).

Line a baking sheet with parchment paper and arrange slices of bacon on sheet without overlapping. Bacon may be cooked in batches depending on the size of the oven and baking sheet(s).

Place baking sheet in oven and cook for 3 to 5 minutes or until bacon is crisp and sticky. Rotate baking sheet as necessary; bacon will darken and can burn quickly if not attended. Remove baking sheet from oven and allow bacon to cool to room temperature on baking sheet.

Once bacon is cooled, either use immediately or place in an airtight container and store for up to 2 weeks in the refrigerator.

 If using from refrigerator, gently warm the bacon in the oven on low heat (around 220°F/100°C) for 2 to 3 minutes before using.

→→ MAKES APPROX. 30 SLICES ←←

FRIED SHALLOTS

20 red shallots
4 cups (1 L) canola oil
kosher salt, to taste
small piece of soft bread

Using a sharp knife, finely slice shallots, on the grain, in half length-wise. Set aside at room temperature.

In a large pot, heat oil to 350°F (180°C).

Place shallots in a fine sieve and carefully submerge sieve into the hot oil, allowing oil to cover the shallots. Cook shallots for 3 to 10 seconds.

 Be very careful as the shallots contain a lot of moisture that will react with the oil and potentially bubble and spit.

Lift sieve from oil and rest sieve over a heat-proof pot or bowl to catch excess oil. Allow pot of oil to return to 350°F (180°C). Repeat process until the moisture has been cooked from the shallots and the oil no longer reacts.

Once the oil accepts the shallots without reacting, carefully empty the shallots from the sieve into the oil. Using a slotted stainless steel spoon, carefully stir shallots gently and deep-fry for 5 to 10 minutes or until light golden brown.

Carefully pour the hot oil through a sieve into a heat-proof pot or container to remove the fried shallots. Place fried shallots on a thin layer of paper towel to absorb excess oil and to speed up the cooling process. Lightly sprinkle fried shallots with salt.

In an airtight container, place a folded square of paper towel and a small piece of bread in the bottom. Top bread with fried shallots and store in a dry, cool place for up to 3 days.

 Shallots will lose crispness if stored for longer than 3 days.

→ MAKES 1 CUP (250 ML) ←

FRIED GARLIC

50 cloves elephant garlic, peeled
4 cups (1 L) whole milk (approx.)
4 cups (1 L) canola oil
small piece of soft bread

> Prepare garlic 1 day ahead
> of cooking.
>
> Elephant garlic is a variant
> of the garden leek family,
> which forms a garlic-like bulb.
> Elephant garlic is much milder
> in flavour than regular garlic.

Using a sharp knife, roughly chop garlic into smaller pieces until it is consistently fine. Do not use a garlic press, as the garlic will lose its texture. Place garlic in a medium bowl and cover with milk. Stir to distribute garlic, and cover bowl with plastic wrap. Place in refrigerator overnight.

In a large, heavy-bottomed pot, heat oil to 350°F (180°F).

Strain garlic through a fine sieve, and rinse thoroughly under cold running water. Empty sieve of garlic onto paper towel, and pat garlic dry, removing as much moisture as possible.

Place garlic into a heatproof sieve, and carefully lower sieve into hot oil to cook garlic briefly. Be careful, as the oil will react to the remaining moisture in the garlic and bubble up. After 5 seconds, remove sieve and drain over a heat-proof container. Allow oil to settle, and return to temperature. Return sieve of garlic to the oil for a further 5 seconds. Repeat this process until the oil does not react to the moisture in the garlic. Deep-fry garlic until just golden brown and void of moisture. Remove sieve from oil and allow fried garlic to drain over a heat-proof container. Spread fried garlic onto a paper towel to absorb excess oil.

Store on fresh paper towel in an airtight container with a piece of soft bread off to the side for up to 1 week or as long as the garlic remains crispy.

→→ MAKES ½ CUP (125 ML) ←←

FURIKAKE

10 sheets nori (Japanese seaweed)
3 Tbsp (45 mL) mixed toasted sesame seeds
1 Tbsp (15 mL) fine sugar
1 tsp (5 mL) sea salt
¼ tsp (1 mL) Schichimi Togarashi

> Nori (Japanese seaweed),
> mixed toasted sesame seeds
> (white and black), and Schi-
> chimi Togarashi can be found
> at most Asian food stores.

Furikake is a Japanese rice seasoning. I've found that it is very versatile and love using it for seasoning Japanese-inspired tacos.

In a food processor, pulse nori until fine. Transfer to a bowl and combine with remaining ingredients.

Transfer to an airtight container and store at room temperature for up to 3 months.

→→ MAKES ½ CUP (125 ML) ←←

CORN TORTILLAS

4 cups (1 L) masa flour (approx.)
1 tsp (5 mL) kosher salt
4 cups (1 L) water (approx.)
¼ cup (60 mL) canola oil, for brushing

You will need a tortilla press, which is available at Latin grocers and specialty retailers. I prefer to use Maseca brand masa flour, which is available at many major grocers. Masa flour is also available at most Latin grocers.

Tortillas should be made just prior to serving.

Like with any dough, the humidity on a given day will determine how much water is required to mix through the masa flour when making Corn Tortillas. Add water gradually, until the dough holds together.

In a bowl, whisk flour and salt together. Add water, and knead until dough is firm and springy. Dough should err on the side of looking dry as opposed to wet. Place 2 heaping tablespoons (30+ mL) of dough in your hands, and form into a ball. Place ball in the centre of a tortilla press lined with plastic wrap. If the dough crumbles after pressing, it is too dry; add a small amount of water to the dough and knead to combine. If the dough sticks to the press, it is too wet; add a small amount of flour to the dough mixture and knead to combine.

Heat a cast iron skillet or flat griddle on high, and brush with oil. While skillet is heating, continue to press tortillas, covering pressed tortillas with a clean dry tea towel as you go.

Cook tortillas in batches by placing them on the oiled skillet and cooking for 1 to 2 minutes or until slightly charred. Flip tortillas and cook for an additional 15 to 20 seconds. Transfer to a tortilla holder or cover with a clean dry tea towel as you go.

Serve family-style from a tortilla holder or tea towel, or plate individually with taco fillings.

→ MAKES 24 TORTILLAS ←

PITA BREAD

1¼ cups (310 mL) tepid water

1½ tsp (7 mL) active dry yeast

1½ tsp (7 mL) superfine sugar

2 cups (500 mL) all-purpose flour

½ tsp (2 mL) sea salt

½ cup (125 mL) + ¼ cup (60 mL) olive oil
(approx.), divided

You can make the Pita Bread days in advance if you wish. They freeze fantastically well and defrost quickly. Just gently warm in the oven before serving. If you have any left over, brush them with herb oil and toast them gently in the oven until crisp. Break them up into pieces and throw them in a salad. Perfect for Fattoush (page 17).

In a bowl, combine water, yeast, and sugar. Mix well, and then set aside in a warm spot until mixture foams, approximately 20 minutes.

In a large bowl, combine flour and salt. Mix well, and then make a well in the centre of the mixture. Add ½ cup (125 mL) oil and yeast mixture, and combine. Work the mixture until it comes together and then turn out onto a lightly floured work surface and knead for a few minutes until dough becomes silky and smooth.

Put dough back into the bowl and cover with a tea towel. Set aside at room temperature and allow dough to rise for 15 to 20 minutes.

Preheat the barbecue to medium heat, approximately 300°F (150°C).

Divide the dough into 12 equal portions, and roll each into flat, thin, even disks, approximately 6 inches (16 cm) in diameter.

Brush the flat bread with remaining oil, and place oil side down on the barbecue. Gently brush a little oil on top as well. In a matter of seconds the bread will start to puff, and after 20 to 25 seconds flip them over and cook for an additional 20 seconds.

NOTE *Do not cook for too long or they will dry out and become crisp.*

When flat breads are cooked, stack them one on top of the other and wrap tightly in a clean tea towel or plastic wrap to keep them warm and soft until ready to use.

→ MAKES 12 ←

STEAMED BUNS

½ Tbsp (7 mL) fine sugar
1 cup (250 mL) lukewarm water
½ Tbsp (7 mL) active dry yeast
1 Tbsp (15 mL) sesame oil
½ Tbsp (7 mL) baking powder
1⅔ cups (410 mL) all-purpose flour
canola oil, for greasing foil

Like making dumplings, making steamed buns from scratch can be a bit time-consuming, so it is recommended that you double, triple, or even quadruple this recipe to make a large batch and freeze leftover steamed buns (not raw, uncooked dough) for later use.

Place sugar and water in a mixing bowl and stir until sugar dissolves. Add yeast and let rest until the mixture is frothy, approximately 10 minutes.

Add sesame oil, baking powder, and flour. Stir the mixture with your hands until it comes together as a smooth, slightly wet dough. Cover bowl with a damp cloth or plastic wrap and allow the dough to rise at room temperature.

 The time for dough rising will vary greatly depending on your kitchen's conditions, but could take 30 minutes to 2 hours.

When the dough has doubled in size, knock it back with your fist and scrape it out of the bowl. Roll the dough into a log shape approximately 1½ inches (4 cm) in diameter. Cut log into pieces approximately 1½ inches (4 cm) wide to form individual buns. Place buns on a tray and cover with a damp towel or plastic wrap. Allow to rise again at room temperature until doubled in size.

Create squares of foil large enough to cover most of the surface area of your steamer baskets, leaving some openings around the edges of the foil to allow steam to reach the buns. Lightly brush the foil squares with canola oil. Set up your steamer with the foil-lined baskets over a pot filled with 2 inches (5 cm) of hot water. Heat water to a simmer over medium-high heat.

Place buns on oiled foil squares in the steamer baskets so that they are not touching. Steam for 12 to 15 minutes or until buns are cooked. Remove from steamer, and serve immediately.

→ MAKES 12 BUNS ←

CURRIES

The following curry paste recipes are used in multiple ways throughout this book, from flavouring soups and fish cakes to their primary use as the base for curries. Throughout Southeast Asia, curries are most often wet pastes, cooked with coconut milk; curries in the Indian subcontinent are more often a dry blend cooked with crushed tomatoes or yogurt. The following curry paste recipes include two from Thailand (red and green curry pastes) and one from Indonesia (Rendang curry).

MADRAS CURRY PASTE

2 red shallots, roughly chopped

4 cloves garlic

1.5-inches (4 cm) long piece ginger, peeled and roughly chopped

¾ cup (185 mL) malt vinegar

¼ cup (60 mL) ground cumin

1 Tbsp (15 mL) black mustard seeds

½ cup (125 mL) ground coriander

1 Tbsp (15 mL) ground turmeric

1 Tbsp (15 mL) garam masala

1 tsp (5 mL) ground cinnamon

1 Tbsp (15 mL) chili powder

1 Tbsp (15 mL) freshly ground black pepper

1 Tbsp (15 mL) kosher salt

½ cup (125 mL) canola oil

In a blender, combine shallots, garlic, ginger, and vinegar. Purée until very smooth, and set aside at room temperature.

In a bowl, combine all of the spices and salt. Add the vinegar mixture, and stir to combine well. Set aside at room temperature.

In a medium pot, heat oil over medium heat. Stir the curry mixture into the oil until oil begins to boil and separate from the spice mix. Remove from heat and allow to cool at room temperature.

Use immediately or transfer to an airtight container and store in the refrigerator indefinitely.

→ MAKES 2 CUPS (500 ML) ←

RED CURRY PASTE

1 Tbsp (15 mL) shrimp paste

5 dried long red chilies

6 shallots, roughly chopped

6 cloves garlic, roughly chopped

2-inch (5 cm) long piece ginger, peeled and roughly chopped

2-inch (5 cm) long piece galangal, peeled and roughly chopped

1 stalk lemongrass, finely sliced

6 kaffir lime leaves, spines removed and roughly chopped

2 bird's eye chilies, roughly chopped (optional, depending on your heat preference)

5 cilantro roots, roughly chopped

1 Tbsp (15 mL) coriander seeds

¼ tsp (1 mL) ground star anise

Preheat oven to 350°F (180°C).

Wrap the shrimp paste in foil and place in oven on baking sheet or directly on rack, roasting for 15 minutes or until dry and aromatic. Remove from oven, and set aside, on the foil, at room temperature.

Soak dried chilies in a bowl of warm water for approximately 10 minutes to rehydrate. Remove from water, pat dry, and roughly chop.

In a blender or using a mortar and pestle, combine all ingredients, and purée until smooth.

Use immediately or store in an airtight container in the refrigerator for up to 1 week.

→» MAKES 2 CUPS (500 ML) «←

RENDANG CURRY PASTE

15 dried red long Thai chilies, seeded

1 stick cinnamon

2 whole cloves

4 whole star anise

2 whole cardamom pods

1 Tbsp (15 mL) shrimp paste

8 kaffir lime leaves, spines removed

6 red shallots, roughly chopped

2⅓-inches (6 cm) long piece ginger, peeled and roughly chopped

3 stalks lemongrass (white parts only), roughly chopped

6 cloves garlic

2⅓-inches (6 cm) long piece galangal, peeled and roughly chopped

1 cup (250 mL) fine unsweetened shredded coconut, toasted

Soak chilies in a bowl of warm water for 20 minutes to rehydrate, and set aside. Remove from water, pat dry, and roughly chop.

In a dry pan, toast cinnamon, cloves, star anise, and cardamom over medium heat for 5 minutes or until aromatic. Stir constantly to avoid burning. Remove from heat and allow spices to cool completely at room temperature.

Once cooled, finely grind toasted spices in a clean spice grinder. Set aside.

Preheat oven to 350°F (180°C).

Spread shrimp paste thinly on a folded piece of foil, and place in the oven. Bake for 5 to 10 minutes or until shrimp paste is aromatic and dry. Remove from oven, and set aside to cool, on the foil, at room temperature.

Place all ingredients except for coconut in a food processor, and purée until smooth. Transfer mixture to a bowl. Add coconut, and mix to combine thoroughly.

Use immediately or transfer to an airtight container and store in the refrigerator for up to 1 month.

→» MAKES 2 CUPS (500 ML) «←

GREEN CURRY PASTE

1 Tbsp (15 mL) shrimp paste

8 dried green long Thai chilies

5 fresh green long Thai chilies

8 shallots, roughly chopped

6 cloves garlic, roughly chopped

2-inches (5 cm) long piece ginger, peeled and roughly chopped

2-inches (5 cm) long piece galangal, peeled and roughly chopped

1 stalk lemongrass, finely sliced

6 kaffir lime leaves, spines removed and roughly chopped

2 green bird's eye chilies (optional, depending on your heat preference)

5 cilantro roots, stems and leaves, roughly chopped

1 Tbsp (15 mL) ground coriander

¼ tsp (1 mL) ground star anise

Preheat oven to 350°F (180°C).

Wrap the shrimp paste in foil, place in oven on baking sheet or directly on rack, and roast for 15 minutes or until dry and aromatic. Remove from oven and set aside, on the foil, at room temperature.

Soak dried long green Thai chilies in a bowl of warm water for approximately 10 minutes to rehydrate. Remove from water, pat dry, and roughly chop.

Place all ingredients into a blender (or mortar and pestle), and purée until smooth.

Use immediately or store in an airtight container in the refrigerator for up to 1 week.

→ MAKES 2 CUPS (500 ML) ←

BROWN CHICKEN STOCK

2 whole chicken carcasses

¼ cup (60 mL) tomato paste

2 cups (500 mL) red wine

1 cup (250 mL) port

1 cup (250 mL) cream sherry

2 stalks celery

1 yellow onion

2-inches (5 cm) long piece ginger, peeled

½ cup cilantro roots, soaked in cold water

1 bulb garlic, cut in half horizontally

2 Tbsp (30 mL) thyme leaves

1.5 gal. (6 L) water

Preheat oven to 350°F (180°C).

Clean excess fat from chicken carcasses. Place carcasses in a deep roasting pan and roast in the oven for approximately 1 hour. After the first hour, spread the tomato paste on the carcasses in the roasting pan and continue to roast for an additional 30 minutes or until carcasses are completely golden brown. Remove carcasses from oven and place in a large stock pot, reserving roasting pan.

Place the red wine, port, and sherry into the reserved pan. To deglaze, use a wooden spoon to scratch and lift the drippings from the bottom of the pan, pouring the contents into the stock pot.

Roughly chop celery, onion, and ginger, and add to the stock pot along with cilantro roots, garlic, and thyme. Gently add water, and bring to a simmer over high heat. It is important that you do not allow the stock to boil or stir the stock as this will make it cloudy. While stock is coming to a simmer, use a ladle to skim any impurities and fat that rise to the surface and discard.

Once stock reaches a simmer, reduce heat to low to achieve a very gentle bubble. Cook for 12 hours. Without stirring, continue to periodically skim any impurities from the surface of the stock during this cooking time.

Pour stock through a fine sieve into an airtight container. Set up an ice bath large enough to hold your container. Rapidly cool container in ice bath, whisking the stock to bring the temperature down as quickly as possible. Seal container, and store in the freezer for up to 6 months or in the refrigerator for up to 1 week.

→→ MAKES 24 CUPS (6 L) ←←

CHICKEN STOCK

2 whole chicken carcasses

2 stalks celery

1 yellow onion

2-inches (5 cm) long piece ginger, peeled

2 cups (500 mL) cilantro with roots

1 bulb garlic, cut in half horizontally

2 Tbsp (30 mL) thyme leaves

1.5 gal (6 L) water

Under cold running water, rinse chicken carcasses and remove excess fat. Place carcasses in a large stock pot.

Roughly chop celery, onion, and ginger, and add to the stock pot along with cilantro, garlic, and thyme. Gently add water, and bring to a simmer over high heat. Do not allow stock to boil. While stock is coming to a simmer, use a ladle to skim any impurities and fat that rise to the surface and discard.

Once stock reaches a simmer, reduce heat to low to achieve a very gentle bubble. Cook for 12 hours. Continue to periodically skim any impurities from the surface of the stock during this cooking time. It is important that you do not allow the stock to boil or stir the stock as this will make it cloudy.

Pour stock through a fine sieve into an airtight container. Set up an ice bath large enough to hold your container. Rapidly cool container in ice bath, whisking the stock to bring the temperature down as quickly as possible. Seal container, and store in the freezer for up to 6 months or in the refrigerator for up to 1 week.

→ MAKES 20 CUPS (5 L) ←

MASTER STOCK

1.25 gal (5 L) water
6 cups (1.5 L) Shaoxing cooking wine
1 cup (250 mL) light soy sauce
⅓ cup (80 mL) fish sauce
2-inches (5 cm) long piece ginger, peeled
2-inches (5 cm) long piece galangal, peeled
1 stalk lemongrass
8 red shallots
10 red long Thai chilies
1 bulb garlic, cut in half horizontally
4 kaffir lime leaves
5 whole star anise
1 stick cinnamon
1 black cardamom pod

> Shaoxing cooking wine is
> a Chinese cooking wine,
> available at Asian grocers and
> most major supermarkets.

A master stock is a stock that is used repeatedly for braising or poaching meats. It is never discarded; in addition to taking on the flavours of the cooked proteins, it is constantly topped up with fresh aromatics, and reused time after time. Generations of chefs have passed on master stocks that are still in use today, much like bread starters that have been fed and passed down through generations of bread makers. Once used, the stock must be chilled rapidly and stored properly either in the refrigerator or freezer, and re-boiled before use. If storing in the refrigerator, it must be used within three days. If you're not planning on using it regularly, it is best to chill the stock and store it in the freezer until your next use.

In a large stock pot, combine all liquids.

Roughly chop ginger, galangal, lemongrass, shallots, and chilies, and add to stock pot.

Add remaining ingredients to stock pot and bring to a boil over high heat. Reduce heat to low and gently simmer for 1 hour. Remove from heat and allow to cool at room temperature.

Pour stock through a fine sieve into an airtight container and place in the refrigerator to cool completely.

Store in the refrigerator for up to 3 days between uses. If not using regularly, store in the freezer for up to 3 months between uses.

→ MAKES 27 CUPS (6.75 L) ←

VEAL STOCK

8.8 lb (4 kg) veal bones
¼ cup (60 mL) tomato paste
2 cups (500 mL) red wine
1 cup (250 mL) port
1 cup (250 mL) cream sherry
1 carrot
2 stalks celery
1 yellow onion
2-inch (5 cm) long piece ginger, peeled
1 bulb garlic, cut in half horizontally
1 Tbsp (15 mL) thyme leaves
2 Tbsp (30 mL) rosemary leaves
1.5 gal (6 L) water

You can ask most butchers for veal bones.

Preheat oven to 350°F (180°C).

Place veal bones in a deep roasting pan and roast in the oven for approximately 1 hour. Spread the tomato paste on the veal bones in the pan and continue to roast for an additional 30 minutes or until bones are completely golden brown. Remove bones from oven and place in a large stock pot, reserving roasting pan.

Place the red wine, port, and sherry into reserved pan. To deglaze, use a wooden spoon to scratch and lift the drippings from the bottom of the pan, pouring the contents into the stock pot.

Roughly chop carrot, celery, onion, and ginger, and add to the stock pot along with garlic, thyme, and rosemary. Gently add water and bring to a simmer over high heat. Do not allow stock to boil. While stock is coming to a simmer, use a ladle to skim any impurities and fat that rise to the surface and discard.

Once stock reaches a simmer, reduce heat to low to achieve a very gentle bubble and allow to cook for 10 to 12 hours. Without stirring, continue to periodically skim any impurities from the surface of the stock during this cooking time. It is important that you do not allow stock to boil or stir the stock as this will make it cloudy.

Pour stock through a fine sieve into an airtight container. Set up an ice bath large enough to hold your container. Rapidly cool container in ice bath, whisking the stock to bring the temperature down as quickly as possible. Seal container, and store in the freezer for up to 6 months or in the refrigerator for up to 1 week.

⇒ MAKES 24 CUPS (6 L) ⇐

SAUCES

CHERRY GASTRIQUE

1 cup (250 mL) white vinegar
2 cups (500 mL) fresh cherries,
  pitted, divided
1 cup (250 mL) superfine sugar

In a food processor, combine vinegar and 1 cup (250 mL) of cherries. Pulse to break up cherries into large pieces.

Transfer contents to a medium pot, and add sugar and remaining 1 cup (250 mL) of cherries. Bring mixture to a boil over high heat, stirring constantly to dissolve sugar. Reduce heat to medium, and simmer for 15 to 20 minutes or until liquid has reduced and is thick and syrupy. Remove from heat and allow to cool completely at room temperature.

Use immediately or transfer to an airtight container and store in the refrigerator for up to 3 months.

→ MAKES 1 1/2 CUPS (375 ML) ←

CHILI CARAMEL

1¾ cups (435 mL) palm sugar, shaved
¾ cup (185 mL) water
4 bird's eye chilies, finely sliced
2 red long Thai chilies, finely sliced
fish sauce, to taste

In a small pot, dissolve palm sugar in water over high heat. Add chilies. Bring to a boil, and then reduce heat to medium and simmer for 10 minutes or until liquid has reduced and thickened. Remove from heat and allow to cool slightly at room temperature.

Slowly whisk fish sauce into chili caramel. Allow to cool completely, transfer to an airtight container, and store in the refrigerator for up to 1 month.

→ MAKES 1 1/2 CUPS (375 ML) ←

AIOLI/MAYONNAISE

2 cloves garlic
kosher salt, to taste
2 egg yolks
¼ cup (60 mL) white vinegar
¾ cup (185 mL) grape seed oil
juice of ½ lemon

> Important: To make mayonnaise, omit the garlic from the recipe.

Using a mortar and pestle, finely crush garlic. Add a pinch of salt (used as an abrasive). Mix well, and set aside at room temperature.

In a food processor, combine egg yolks, vinegar, and finely crushed garlic. While puréeing, add oil in a slow, steady stream. Continue puréeing until mixture emulsifies.

 Feel free to stop pouring oil at any time to catch up with combining the mixture.

Carefully add lemon juice bit by bit to the mixture and season with salt to achieve desired flavour.

Use immediately or transfer to an airtight container and store in the refrigerator for up to 2 weeks.

→→ MAKES 1 CUP (250 ML) ←←

CHILI JAM

10 dried red long Thai chilies, seeded
2 Tbsp (30 mL) shrimp paste
2 Tbsp (30 mL) dried shrimp
⅓ cup (80 mL) peanut oil
12 red long Thai chilies, seeded and
   finely chopped
5 red shallots, finely chopped
5 cloves garlic, finely chopped
2-inches (5 cm) piece galangal, peeled
   and finely chopped
2-inches (5 cm) piece ginger, peeled and
   finely chopped
30 cherry tomatoes, halved
½ cup (125 mL) tamarind water
1½ Tbsp (22 mL) fish sauce (approx.)
⅔ cup (160 mL) palm sugar,
   shaved (approx.)

Preheat oven to 350°F (180°C).

Soak chilies in a bowl of warm water for 30 minutes and finely chop. Set aside at room temperature.

Wrap shrimp paste and dried shrimp separately in foil and place in oven. Roast for 15 minutes or until fragrant. Remove from oven, and set aside, on the foil, at room temperature.

In a large saucepan, heat oil over medium heat and sauté chilies, shallots, garlic, galangal, and ginger for 10 minutes or until fragrant and beginning to brown. Reduce heat to low and add tomatoes, roasted shrimp paste, roasted dried shrimp, and tamarind water. Combine well. Increase heat to medium and cook for approximately 10 minutes, stirring well.

Remove mixture from heat, and place contents in a blender. Purée until very smooth, and then transfer contents back to saucepan. Add the fish sauce and palm sugar, and cook for approximately 1 minute over medium heat. Taste for a balance of flavours, adjusting if necessary. Remove from heat, and allow to cool at room temperature.

Use immediately or transfer to an airtight container and store in the refrigerator for up to 2 weeks.

→→ MAKES 4 CUPS (1 L) ←←

CHILI MINT RELISH

2 cups (500 mL) mint leaves
1 batch Mint Gastrique (recipe follows)
½ cup (125 mL) flat leaf parsley leaves
1 bunch green onions
2 bird's eye chilies, seeded

Reserve half of the stems from the mint leaves for the Mint Gastrique. You can make the Mint Gastrique at this point, and set aside at room temperature to cool before you proceed with making the Chili Mint Relish.

Once the Mint Gastrique has cooled to room temperature, pick parsley leaves and discard stems. Set aside at room temperature.

Cut the green tops off the onions and reserve the white ends for a later use. Roughly chop green tops and place in a blender. Add mint, parsley, chilies, and Mint Gastrique. Purée on high speed until very smooth.

Ideally, Chili Mint Relish should be used immediately as it discolours quickly. Alternatively, it can be stored in an airtight container in the refrigerator for no longer than 2 days.

→→ MAKES 2 CUPS (500 ML) ←←

MINT GASTRIQUE

¾ cup (185 mL) fine sugar
¾ cup (185 mL) white vinegar
stems from 1 cup (250 mL) mint leaves

In a small pot, combine all ingredients and slowly bring to a boil over medium-high heat. Once sugar has dissolved completely, reduce heat to medium, and simmer for 10 to 15 minutes or until syrupy. Remove from heat, and allow to cool completely.

Use immediately or transfer to an airtight container and store in the refrigerator for up to 3 months.

→→ MAKES 1 ¼ CUPS (310 ML) ←←

CHILI TAMARIND

1 tsp (5 mL) shrimp paste
10 red long Thai chilies, divided
2-inches (5 cm) long piece ginger, peeled
2 cloves garlic
5 red shallots
1 Tbsp (15 mL) grape seed oil
2 cups (500 mL) tamarind water
⅔ cup (160 mL) palm sugar,
  shaved (approx.)
fish sauce, to taste

Preheat oven to 350°F (180°C).

Spread shrimp paste on a piece of foil and loosely wrap. Roast in the oven for 20 minutes or until dry. Remove from oven, and set aside, on the foil, at room temperature.

Remove and discard the seeds from 5 of the chilies, and set chilies aside.

Roughly chop ginger, garlic, shallots, and all chilies. Set aside at room temperature.

In a medium pot, heat oil over high heat. Add chopped ingredients and gently fry over medium-high heat for 5 minutes or until caramelized. Add roasted shrimp paste, tamarind water, and palm sugar. Bring to a boil, then reduce heat to low and gently cook for 15 minutes or until jammy. Remove from heat, and season with fish sauce and more palm sugar, to taste.

Transfer mixture to a food processor and purée until smooth. Pass mixture through a fine sieve into a bowl or resealable container, gently pushing with the back of a ladle, and discard contents in the sieve.

Use immediately or cover and store in the refrigerator for up to 1 month.

→ MAKES 2¾ CUPS (685 ML) ←

GUACAMOLE

3 ripe avocados
½ medium red onion, finely diced
juice of 3 limes
kosher salt, to taste

In a medium bowl, place flesh of avocadoes and mash. Set aside pits. Add onion and lime juice, and mix to combine. Season with salt.

Use immediately or transfer to an airtight container, placing avocado pits in the mixture and covering the surface with plastic wrap. Store in the refrigerator for up to 1 week.

NOTE *The discoloured surface of the guacamole can be removed, if needed.*

→ MAKES 2 CUPS (500 ML) ←

HOT SMOKED PINEAPPLE AND HABANERO HOT SAUCE

1 large pineapple

8 habanero peppers, stems removed

4 cloves garlic

3 shallots

1 cup (250 mL) superfine sugar (approx.)

1 cup (250 mL) white vinegar (approx.)

2 mangos, peeled and roughly chopped

1 ripe papaya, peeled and roughly chopped

cilantro roots, washed thoroughly

kosher salt, to taste

> This recipe yields a large batch of hot sauce, as there is no point in setting up a hot smoker to make a small batch. Sauce can be jarred for long-term storage or stored in an airtight container in refrigerator. Set up water tray to catch drippings and encapsulate smoke.

Preheat smoker or barbecue to 425°F (220°F).

Place a heat-proof tray, three-quarters full of cold water, into the bottom of the smoker or barbecue set up for hot smoking.

 Monitor water tray throughout smoking process to ensure it doesn't dry out. Top up with water as needed.

Place pineapple, skin on, in hot smoker or barbecue and smoke for 4 hours. Add habaneros, garlic, and shallots to the smoker and smoke with the pineapple for an additional 2 hours. Remove ingredients from smoker, and set aside at room temperature.

Remove heat-proof tray from smoker, and strain any solids or impurities from the smoked water into a large saucepan. Add sugar and vinegar to the water. Bring to a boil over high heat. Once boiling, reduce heat to medium, and simmer for 30 minutes or until liquid has reduced by half.

With a sharp knife, remove outer skin from pineapple. Cut pineapple into quarters lengthwise, and remove core. Roughly chop pineapple flesh.

In a blender or food processor, working in batches, purée smoked pineapple, habaneros, garlic, and shallots with mango, papaya, and cilantro roots, adding small amounts of smoked water-vinegar mixture to each batch just to help purée the solids. Purée until smooth, repeating this process until everything is puréed. Between each batch, empty purée into a large bowl. Season with salt, and, if needed, add more sugar and vinegar to achieve a balance of saltiness, sourness, and sweetness.

Transfer sauce into sterilized canning jars and store in the refrigerator for up to 12 months. If possible, allow for 2 weeks of aging in the jar before use.

→ MAKES 8 CUPS (2 L) ←

LABNE

4 cups (1 L) full-fat plain yogurt
1 tsp (5 mL) kosher salt

> Seek out a quality, full-fat plain yogurt.
>
> You will need clean fine cheesecloth and butcher's twine.

Labne is essentially a yogurt cheese. It can be used to make dips and yogurt sauces or, when hung for a longer period of time to remove more liquid, it can be used to make *labne* cheese balls that can be stored and marinated for future use. The possible flavour combinations are endless; use your imagination and have fun.

In a bowl, combine yogurt and salt. Mix thoroughly.

Place a square piece of cheesecloth in the bottom of a small bowl and spoon yogurt mixture into the centre of the cheesecloth. Bring the four corners of the cheesecloth together to form an enclosed sack and tie with butcher's twine.

Tie the closed end of the yogurt sack to a long-handled wooden spoon, and suspend it above a container in the refrigerator. Be sure to leave approximately 4 inches (10 cm) of space between the bottom of the yogurt sack and the bottom of the container to allow liquid to drain from the yogurt. Leave to hang for approximately 8 hours to achieve *labne*.

 NOTE *You can leave it hanging in the refrigerator for 24–72 hours to achieve yogurt cheese. The longer the yogurt hangs, the firmer the cheese becomes.*

Once *labne* reaches desired firmness it is ideal to use immediately in the recipe of your choice. However, you can transfer it to an airtight container and store in the refrigerator for up to 1 month.

» MAKES 4 CUPS (1 L) «

NUOC MAM

2 cups (500 mL) fish sauce

6 Tbsp fine sugar, to taste (approx.)

1 carrot, grated

5 cloves garlic, finely chopped

2 bird's eye chilies, finely chopped

lemon juice, to taste

lime juice, to taste

Nuoc Mam is a Vietnamese dipping sauce, often served with spring rolls and rice paper rolls.

In a plastic or glass container with a lid, combine all of the ingredients and shake gently to combine.

 There should be a balance of salty, sweet, and citrus when tasted. Adjust flavours, if necessary.

Transfer to an airtight container and store in the refrigerator for up to 3 weeks.

→ MAKES 2 CUPS (500 ML) ←

PINE NUT SKORDALIA

1 cup (250 mL) pine nuts

12 cloves garlic

3 egg yolks

⅓ cup (80 mL) white wine vinegar

⅓ cup (80 mL) lemon juice

2 ⅓ cups (580 mL) sunflower oil

kosher salt, to taste

black pepper, freshly cracked, to taste

Skordalia is a thick, emulsified dip made in a style similar to mayonnaise.

In a dry pan, toast pine nuts over medium-high heat for 5 minutes or until golden brown, tossing continually to ensure pine nuts do not burn. Remove from heat, and place toasted pine nuts in a food processor. Add garlic, egg yolks, white wine vinegar, and lemon juice. Purée until smooth. Continue to purée while very gradually trickling oil into the mixture. Once combined, transfer contents to a bowl, and season with salt and pepper.

Use immediately or transfer to an airtight container and store in the refrigerator for up to 2 weeks.

→ MAKES 4 CUPS (1 L) ←

SMOKED TOMATO AIOLI

2 cups (500 mL) hickory smoking chips
1 red bell pepper
2 Roma tomatoes, halved lengthwise
8 cloves garlic
6 red shallots
2 bird's eye chilies
2 cups (500 mL) water
1 batch Mayonnaise (page 266)
Worcestershire sauce, to taste

Set up a hot smoker to manufacturer's instructions using hickory smoking chips, and set temperature for 210°F (100°C). If you do not have a hot smoker, refer to page 282 for hot smoking with a barbecue.

Place red pepper, tomatoes, garlic, shallots, and chilies in the hot smoker, and smoke for 2 hours.

Regardless of your smoking technique, place a heat-proof tray with cold water underneath the ingredients to catch drippings and encapsulate the smoke.

Remove smoked vegetables from the hot smoker or barbecue, and place in a food processor. Purée the ingredients until smooth, and transfer to a medium pot. Strain any solids or impurities from the water in the catchment tray into the pot with the puréed mixture.

Bring mixture to a simmer over high heat; reduce heat to low, and cook for 90 minutes or until liquid is reduced to a jam-like consistency. Remove from heat, and push the mixture through a fine sieve with the back of a ladle. Set aside, and allow to cool to room temperature. Once cooled, place in the refrigerator and allow to cool completely.

Place Mayonnaise in a bowl, and gradually fold in smoked mixture until aioli reaches desired consistency. Gradually add Worcestershire sauce. Stir to combine.

Use immediately or transfer to an airtight container and store in the refrigerator for up to 1 month.

→ MAKES 2½ CUPS (625 ML) ←

TARRAGON DRESSING

2 cups (500 mL) tarragon leaves
3⅓ Tbsp (50 mL) white sugar
⅓ cup (80 mL) white vinegar
1¼ cups (310 mL) canola oil
kosher salt, to taste

In a blender, combine tarragon, sugar, and vinegar. Blend until combined. While still blending, slowly add oil and blend until emulsified, being careful to not let mixture split. Season with salt.

Use immediately or transfer to an airtight container and store in the refrigerator for up to 1 month.

→ MAKES 2 CUPS (500 ML) ←

TOASTED COCONUT CREAM

½ cup (125 mL) fine unsweetened
  shredded coconut
1 tsp (5 mL) rice flour
1 cup (250 mL) coconut cream, divided
pinch of salt
2 Tbsp (30 mL) white sugar, or more to taste

Toasted Coconut Cream can be served warm or cold.

Preheat oven to 350°F (180°C).

Spread coconut in a thin layer on a baking sheet, and place in oven. Toast for 8 to 10 minutes or until golden brown. Remove from oven, and allow to cool on the baking sheet at room temperature.

In a bowl, mix flour with ¼ cup (60 mL) of coconut cream to form a paste. In a medium saucepan, mix remaining coconut cream with flour paste over medium heat, whisking vigorously to incorporate. Add salt and toasted coconut. Bring to a boil, and cook for approximately 5 minutes, stirring constantly. When coconut cream has thickened, remove from heat immediately. Add sugar, and stir until dissolved. Add additional sugar to reach desired sweetness. Set aside at room temperature to cool.

Use immediately or transfer to an airtight container and store in the refrigerator for up to 1 week.

→→ MAKES 1¾ CUPS (435 ML) ←←

TZATZIKI

2¼-inches (6 cm) long piece English
  cucumber, peeled and seeded
1 cup (250 mL) Labne (page 270)
juice of ½ lemon
2 cloves garlic, crushed
kosher salt, to taste
black pepper, freshly cracked, to taste

Grate the cucumber and place in the centre of a tea towel. Bring the sides of the towel together, and wring very tightly to squeeze out excess liquid.

Place cucumber in a bowl with Labne, lemon juice, and garlic. Season with salt and pepper.

Use immediately or transfer to an airtight container and store in the refrigerator for up to 2 weeks.

→→ MAKES 1 CUP (250 ML) ←←

TOUM

15 cloves garlic
juice of 1 lemon
1 tsp (5 mL) kosher salt
1¼ cups (310 mL) sunflower oil
2 tsp (10 mL) cold water
2 large egg yolks (optional)

Toum is a garlic sauce common throughout Egypt and the eastern Mediterranean. It can be used as a dip, as a spread for sandwiches, or mixed into sauces and marinades.

In a blender, purée garlic, lemon juice, and salt until smooth. While still puréeing, very slowly and gradually pour (almost dripping) oil into mixture, making sure mixture emulsifies between each addition of oil. Continue until all oil has been added. Add cold water, and turn off blender. If mixture splits, remove mixture from blender and clean blender thoroughly. Add 2 egg yolks to blender and purée, slowly adding split mixture to the blender.

Use immediately or transfer to an airtight container and store in the refrigerator for up to 2 weeks.

→→ MAKES 2 CUPS (500 ML) ←←

ZHOUG

2 tsp (10 mL) caraway seeds, toasted
2 cups (500 mL) cilantro leaves
1 clove garlic
1 bird's eye chili, stems removed
3 Tbsp (45 mL) cold water
kosher salt, to taste
black pepper, freshly cracked, to taste

Zhoug is a Middle Eastern condiment, used most commonly in Israel and Yemen. It is a spicy relish of cilantro, chilies, garlic, and caraway. It can be used in many different ways, but it's perfect with fish and meats.

Using a mortar and pestle, finely crush the caraway seeds. Set aside at room temperature.

In a blender, combine cilantro, garlic, chili, and water. Purée until smooth. Transfer mixture to a bowl. Add finely crushed caraways seeds and mix well. Season with salt and pepper.

Use immediately or transfer to an airtight container, cover the surface with plastic wrap, seal, and store in the refrigerator for up to 1 week.

→→ MAKES 1 CUP (250 L) ←←

GLOSSARY

BEER

I LOVE BEER! There are a couple of recipes in this book that use beer as an essential ingredient. The specific beers I have chosen to use are based on their flavour and style, local availability, and because these brands have all been very supportive of not only our business, but the food-truck movement as a whole. If you can't find these brands locally, ask your beer or liquor store to recommend something similar.

BIRD'S EYE CHILI

Bird's eye chilies are used extensively in Thai and Vietnamese cooking. They have a fruity heat to them, measuring about 50,000–100,000 Scoville units (not as hot as a habanero, but hotter than a jalapeño). Bird's eye chilies can be red or green, and are typically less than 2 inches (5 cm) long. If not specified either can be used, although red is more commonly available. Due to their unique flavour and heat profile, bird's eye chilies should not be substituted with any other chili.

CILANTRO

I LOVE CILANTRO! I use a lot of cilantro in my cooking. In North America, I've found most people call the fresh plant "cilantro", and the seeds "coriander". I'm pretty sure North Americans are the only people in the world who do that. I usually use the word "coriander" for the fresh plant, and "coriander seed" for . . . well, the seed. However, in this book, I make the distinction by calling the fresh plant "cilantro" and the seed "coriander".

All parts of the cilantro plant are edible and are used for different reasons. Cilantro roots are integral when making Thai curry pastes, as they have a deeper and more intense flavour than the stem or leaf, contain a lot of nutrients, and don't impart a colour where a colour is not wanted (i.e., when making red curry paste, you don't want it to turn green). If your local supermarket does not sell cilantro with the roots intact, check your local Asian grocer.

COCONUT MILK

If you're not making coconut milk yourself from the actual coconut, I recommend using Aroy-D brand. It is preservative-free, and the quality is very consistent.

FISH AND SEAFOOD

Find a local seafood supplier who knows what they're doing. We're lucky to have The Tide & Vine Oyster Company based in Niagara, and we get all of our seafood through them.

When picking fish, only get the freshest. Ask to smell the fish; if it is fresh, it will smell like the ocean, and not fishy. Look at the fish's eyes: any cloudiness indicates age, so the clearer the eyes, the fresher it is. Check the gills of the fish: they should be wet and bright red or pink in colour. Any discoloration or dryness indicates it is not fresh. I recommend always buying your fish whole and breaking it down yourself. If you don't know how to fillet a fish, there is no better time than now to learn, either through online tutorials or by asking your local fish monger to teach you the basics.

FISH SAUCE

Fish sauce is a salty seasoning liquid made by fermenting fish—usually anchovies—with sea salt. It is used in Thai cooking to achieve a balance of salty (fish sauce), sweet (palm sugar), sour (lime juice), and heat (chilies).

FLEUR DE SEL

See Salt.

FRUIT AND VEGGIES

Dishes that feature fresh fruits and vegetables are always best when they're made in season. I use organic, locally grown produce as often as possible. More and more, it's easier to get varieties that were previously difficult to find in North America (especially in the colder climates here in Canada). Our friend Linda Crago at Tree and Twig Heirloom Vegetable Farm in Wainfleet, Ontario, has a surprising variety of plants on her property. She's got Chinese snake beans, Szechuan buttons (an edible plant with flowers that temporarily numb your tongue!), obscurely hot chilies, dozens of herbs and greens, and hundreds of varieties of heirloom tomatoes. We're lucky to have Linda in such close proximity, and that she loves a growing challenge. If you can't find a farm close to you with these products, try your luck at specialty grocers.

GALANGAL

Galangal resembles the more common ginger root in both looks and flavour, but it has a more potent flavour. If you can't find fresh galangal, check the freezer at your local Asian grocer, where you might find it pre-sliced in a vacuum-sealed package.

KAFFIR LIME LEAF

The leaves of the kaffir lime tree have a uniquely intense flavour and scent that is something like a combination of lime and lemongrass. They are widely used in Southeast Asian cuisine, and are an integral ingredient in many curry pastes and soups. When very finely julienned and sprinkled over dishes, they make for a visually interesting and flavourful garnish.

LEMONGRASS

Lemongrass is native to India and is used in teas as well as soups, curries, and stir-fries. It has a distinctive citrus flavour and a firm, fibrous texture.

LONG THAI CHILI

Long Thai chilies look most similar to Serrano chilies, but are usually thinner and are much hotter; they are usually 3 to 4 inches (8 to 10 cm) long, and can be either red or green. Use red chilies for red curry pastes, and green for green curry pastes. You can dry your own chilies by laying fresh chilies out on a wire rack in a cool, dry area that allows air to circulate around the chilies. Discard any chilies that show signs of rot or mould. Move the chilies around periodically so they dry evenly. Dried chilies can be stored indefinitely in an airtight container at room temperature. You can reconstitute dried chilies by soaking them in warm water for 20 minutes.

MEAT

When it comes to meat, you should be able to trace the animal's life back to the farm. Grass-fed or grain-fed (not corn), and humanely raised, treated, and loved is the only option. Develop a relationship with your butcher or local supplier of fine meats and ask questions. If the animal has not been treated like the family pet, don't eat it! If you're not comfortable with any part of the butchery asked for in a recipe, ask your butcher to do it before picking up your meat.

MIRIN

Mirin is a Japanese rice wine that is very similar to, but sweeter than, sake. It is used to flavour sushi rice and dashi broth, but is quite intense and should be used sparingly so as to not overpower the dish.

OILS

For shallow and deep-frying, I use canola oil. It is affordable and has a higher smoke point compared to other oils like olive, sesame, and most peanut oils. I use sunflower oil throughout this book in dressings and to finish plates. I personally prefer to use Pristine Gourmet Foods virgin oils, as they are locally made in Ontario from non-GMO plants and are full-flavoured and versatile.

Due to its lower smoke point and mild flavour, I use grape seed oil for quick cooking processes like searing meats and in sauces and dressings, such as aioli and à la Grecque dressing.

PALM SUGAR

Palm sugar is a natural, unrefined sugar made from the sap of palm trees. It is usually bought in pucks, and can be grated, chopped, or melted whole, depending on your intended use.

PEPPER

I only use freshly ground pepper. I will use either black peppercorns or a blend of green, red, and black. A good pepper mill is like a knife to a chef. I use Peugeot pepper mills and fresh grind whatever amount I need. If it's an extra large amount I will use a spice grinder. I highly advise against using pre-ground pepper, because the aromas and flavours that are released upon grinding only last a short time. Pre-ground pepper is also often coarser in texture than the fine grind of a good pepper mill.

RIGANI

Rigani is a Greek oregano with a very specific flavour profile, and should not be substituted with fresh or dried Italian oregano. Dried *rigani* can be found in specialty ingredient stores and—sometimes if you're lucky—the supermarket.

SALT

For regular cooking, I always use kosher salt—it is easier to handle than fine table salt, distributes better, and thus makes it easier to control your seasoning. It is also free of the additives found in table salt used to prevent clumping.

Fleur de sel is used as a finishing salt, as it adds a nice crunch and burst of saltiness. *Fleur de sel* is hand harvested, and is thus considered an artisanal product, which is often reflected in its higher price point. Canada is now producing all-natural and sustainable hand-harvested *fleur de sel* off the coast of Vancouver Island.

Coarse sea salt is used in curing (e.g., Lamb Shank Taco, page 191) and preserving (e.g., Preserved Lemons, page 248). Because of the larger grain, coarse sea salt doesn't break down and dissolve as quickly as smaller-grain salts would during the curing or preserving processes.

SHRIMP PASTE

Shrimp paste is a concentrated paste made using salt and fermented ground shrimp. It is an essential ingredients in many curries and soups throughout Thailand and Southeast Asia. Roasting shrimp paste releases a much stronger aroma and more intense flavour than if it used in its moist state.

SUMAC

Sumac is a powder made from dried, crushed sumac berries. It is used heavily throughout the Middle East and North Africa, and is a beautiful, fresh, citrusy addition to spice blends, dressings, seasonings, or just sprinkled directly on salads. You can find it at specialty ingredient stores, Middle Eastern grocery stores, or bulk spice stores.

SUNFLOWER SHOOTS

Sunflower shoots have a lovely, nutty sunflower aroma and taste, and make for a pretty garnish with their thick and broad leaves. They can be tricky to find, but are often available at boutique grocers who carry microgreens.

TAMARIND WATER

Tamarind water/purée can be found at some Asian grocery stores, or can be made by boiling tamarind pulp in water for approximately 30 minutes, mashing the pulp to distribute the flavour, and then passing the pulp through a fine sieve and reserving the liquid.

THAI BASIL

Several recipes call for Thai basil. This is a specific variety of basil used in Southeast Asian cooking. It has an anise-like flavour and tastes very different from Italian basil.

TOBIKO

Tobiko is the Japanese word for flying fish roe. It is most recognized as the tiny coloured pearls that garnish sushi and other Japanese dishes. Natural ingredients are used to colour *tobiko*, such as squid ink (black), yuzu (pale orange), and wasabi (bright green). *Tobiko* has a subtle, salty flavour and fun crunchy texture.

EQUIPMENT

CHEESECLOTH

Cheesecloth, or muslin cloth, is used most frequently in cheesemaking, but also comes in handy for things like steaming couscous and other small-grained pastas. Cheesecloth is available in a variety of grades of weave, from open to extra-fine. For hanging yogurt and to make things like Labne (page 270), I recommend a fine or extra-fine weave.

DIGITAL SCALE

I recommend equipping your kitchen with a basic digital scale, especially if you do a lot of baking or work with dried spices. Weighing dry goods is much more accurate than measuring volumes, so a digital scale comes in handy. Basic scales are available in the homewares section of most major supermarkets and at kitchen supply retailers.

MEAT GRINDER

I always grind my meat fresh; it prevents the opportunity for contamination, and allows me to control the texture and flavourings of the meat when I'm cooking. Some meats are not widely available pre-ground at supermarkets, like pork and lamb, so unless your butcher is grinding the meat to order, having a meat grinder in your kitchen is the best bet.

MORTAR AND PESTLE

A mortar is a sturdy bowl, usually made from stone, ceramic, or hard wood. A pestle is a heavy club-shaped tool that is used to grind ingredients in the mortar bowl. Mortar and pestles date back to 35,000 B.C., and are still common kitchen tools around the world. Grinding your own spices and curry pastes helps maintain the freshness and aromatics of the ingredients, and lets you control the coarseness of the grind. Mortar and pestles are available at most kitchen supply retailers, Asian grocers, and some major supermarkets.

SMOKER

If you do not have access to a hot smoker, you can mimic the effects of hot smoking by making a foil pouch to hold wood chips, and placing it directly on the hot element or coals of a barbecue. If you are smoking with the barbecue method, I recommend soaking half of the wood chips in water for a few minutes, and then combining the wet chips with dry wood chips in the foil package. This method is suitable for smoking things like fruits and vegetables, and small cuts of fish or meat. A proper hot smoker is necessary for things like smoking beef briskets and other large cuts of meat that require more smoking time, as you need precise control over the temperature and smoke levels. Hot smokers and wood chips used in hot smoking are available at most barbecue retailers.

SPIDER SPOON

A spider is a utensil with a large, flat wire-mesh basket at the end of a handle. It is used most often as a skimming tool when making stocks, but can also be used like a slotted spoon to lift food out of hot water or oil.

STEAMER

Bamboo steamer baskets or aluminium steamers (which come with a basin, baskets, and lids) are widely available at Asian grocers and most kitchen supply retailers. If you use a bamboo steamer basket, make sure it fits a pot you have in your kitchen without extending past the rim of the pot too much. The tighter the fit, the more efficient the steamer will be. I recommend using parchment paper or lightly oiled foil in the steamer basket when steaming things like dumplings or *bao* (steamed buns). This helps prevent the steamed dough from sticking to the basket as it cooks. Steamers also come in handy for cooking things like couscous, glutinous rice, and vegetables. To steam small-grain pastas and rices, line the steamer basket with a couple of overlapping layers of cheesecloth first.

ACKNOWLEDGMENTS

Suresh Doss: What can I say!? I think it was meant to be that you came to our launch party for the truck all those years ago. You believed in our business, you believed in my food, and you believed in the food-truck industry! You have done so much for the betterment of the food-truck world in North America. You're a true friend!

Sid Friedman: Sid man! You are one of the most unselfish, hard-working, and dedicated people I have had the privilege of working alongside. You see things that most others don't, and work bloody hard at making them happen. It's been a real blast, mate!

Ontario Food Trucks Association: Our food-truck family, who are as crazy as us and do it for the love of food.

Nick Rundall, Jordie Yow, and the whole team at Whitecap Books: Thank you for the opportunity to share the stories and recipes swirling around in my head, and for your enthusiasm and support through the writing and publishing process.

Caiti McLelland: Thank you for keeping me on track with writing, and for putting in the extra effort to make sense of my thoughts! You are a machine, genius, and gem of a person.

Paul Harber, Nate Young, Andrew McLeod, David and Leigh Watt, Ryan and Bev Crawford, and Erik Peacock: All of you have been such a great support network. Your belief and support of our business has been epic. I am humbled and privileged to work alongside such great chefs and industry folks such as yourselves in this awesome region of Niagara.

Mike McColl: Thank you for your support and willingness to help out whenever we've been in need, and for all of the beautiful photos you've taken of our business and food since day one right through to this book. You are an honorary member of the El Gastró family.

Cindy Arman: Sweetheart, your food makes me smile! You have a true gift! Thanks for all your help, and I look forward to working with you in the future.

Cath Claringbold: Thanks for giving me the opportunity to take my career to the next level all those years ago. You were and still are a true inspiration to me and the cooking world!

Nat Paull: Let's see . . . Gerhard Schtickentappen, Spoonus Maximus, and the rest of the kitchen characters, I miss you! We will cook together again one day, I know it! Thanks for everything, Nat—you're a bloody star!

Robert and Carolyn Griffiths and the boys: From washing pots, and washing floors to starting my apprenticeship and the odd boot up the arse, you taught me so much in the first part of my career. Cheers, mate!

Nick and Sonia Anthony: Thank you for giving me the opportunity to be a part of your kitchen. Working under you both was a great experience, and your knowledge and cooking philosophy taught me a lot.

Scott and Rachelle Vivian, Matty Matheson, and Andrew Richmond: You have all been such avid supporters of the food-truck movement and our business. For that we owe you! Toronto is lucky to have talent such as yours, leading the path for the food scene.

The Boston Beer Company: Thank you for helping with this book, and for your belief and support with the food-truck scene. I look forward to continuing our relationship.

The Tide & Vine Oyster Company: Kat and Mike, you guys are such hard workers. You have so much love for food, the industry, and the people around you! It's been an honour working with and alongside you. We can only go up! Cheers, guys, for your support.

Niagara Oast House Brewers: You guys rock, eh? It's been so much fun working with you since you opened. Kevin's passion shows through in his beer. You guys have something special, and we are lucky to have been a part of that!

The Silversmith Brewing Company: Thank you for giving us the opportunity to set up shop and collaborate with you. It's been a blast, and we can only look forward to what's in store next.

Pristine Gourmet: Thank you, Jason, for making such wonderful products, growing excellent produce, and sharing my vision of celebrating homegrown produce.

Shed Pottery: Thank you for contributing beautiful plateware for this book. You have a true talent. I look forward to building an inspiring relationship with your business.

Rossy Earle: One of the boys in the kitchen, you have made me blush on more than one occasion. You're such a happy and loving person. We love you dearly. Thanks for all your help!

Tiffany Mayer: You have such belief in the region of Niagara. Your non-stop positive approach to the area is fantastic. Thank you for your continued support! It's been a privilege knowing you and feeding you.

Linda Crago: Thank you for all the wonderful produce over the years. We look forward to working with you more often.

Jill and Rob Hynam-Smith, Cam Hynam-Smith, Marty, my Nan and late Pa, my Grandma and late Pop, Wendy Hynam-Smith, Eric and Linda Jensen, Derek Jensen, and my extended family: Thank you to my family on both sides of the globe. Your undying belief, support, generosity, and love is what keeps us going! Things can only get better!

Our wonderful friends, who have given us so much support through the good times and the bad, believed in us when we said what we were going to do, and have hopped on the truck and helped us in a pinch.

Our loyal customers, the Gastrónauts, without whom the business would not exist. We are lucky to have you, and so grateful.

Matty Siscoe and Chrissy Sadowski: We literally couldn't be doing what we're doing in Niagara without you. All the long hours and hard work you did to make it possible for us to be a part of this region is overwhelming! I can never thank you enough!

Very special thanks go to my beautiful wife, Tamara, who has stood by me and put up with all of my shit, and has been such a great support. Without her help, the business and this book would not have been possible. Love you, babe.

PARTNERS

DILLON'S SMALL BATCH DISTILLERS
4833 Tufford Road
Beamsville, Ontario
Canada L0R 1B1
905-563-3030
dillons.ca

NIAGARA OAST HOUSE BREWERS
2017 Niagara Stone Road
Niagara-on-the-Lake, Ontario
Canada L0S 1J0
289-868-9627
oasthousebrewers.ca

PRISTINE GOURMET FOODS
1211 Villa Nova Road
RR 1 Waterford, Ontario
Canada N0E 1Y0
519-443-4658
pristinegourmet.com

THE BOSTON BEER COMPANY
30 Germania Street
Boston, Massachusetts
USA 02130
617-368-5080
samueladams.com

SHED POTTERY
Potter Johann Munro
289-668-1888
shedpottery@gmail.com

SUPICUCU
Chef Rossy Earle
supicucu.com

TREE AND TWIG HEIRLOOM VEGETABLE FARM
74038 Regional Road 45
Wellandport, Ontario
Canada L0R 2J0
905-386-7388
treeandtwig.ca

MONDAY TUESDAY

- CRUMBED PORK TONGUE, FENNEL, CHILLI MINT
- BUN BEAR BAO, OAST BEER
- OCCY, BOILED CHATS, SANTLOUIGE SHOOTS
- CRAB CAKES, HARISSA AIOLI, APPLE DUKKAH
- SOFT SHELL CRAB, PINE NUT SKORDALIA
- DUKKAH CRAB SPRING ROLLS, ZHONG
- BOSTON LAGER STEAMED MUSSELS
- TUNISIAN CARROT SALAD
- TOMATOES + RED ONION SALAD.
- TOM KA GAI
- COCONUT CURRY CORN SOUP
- MARINATED BEEF SALAD
- MASTER STOCK BRAISED PORK HOC
  - P. T. O

INDEX